Sam Atieh

How to Get a College Degree Via the Internet

**The Complete Guide
to Getting Your Undergraduate or Graduate Degree
from the Comfort of Your Home**

PRIMA PUBLISHING

PRIMA PUBLISHING and colophon are registered trademarks of Prima Communications, Inc.

Library of Congress Cataloging-in-Publication Data

Atieh, Sam.
　　How to get a college degree via the Internet: the complete guide to getting your undergraduate or graduate degree from the comfort of your home / Sam Atieh
　　　　p.　cm.
　　Includes index.
　　ISBN 0-7615-1370-1
　　　1. Distance education—United States—Computer-assisted instruction.
　　2. Internet (Computer network) in education—United States. 3. Education, Higher—United States—Computer-assisted instruction. 4. Degrees, Academic—United States. I. Title.
LC5803.C65A85　1998
378.1'754—dc21　　　　　　　　　　　　　　　　　　　　　　98-18722
　　　　　　　　　　　　　　　　　　　　　　　　　　　　　　　　CIP

98 99 00 01 02 BB 10 9 8 7 6 5 4 3 2 1
Printed in the United States of America

How to Order
Single copies may be ordered from Prima Publishing, P.O. Box 1260BK, Rocklin, CA 95677; telephone (916) 632-4400. Quantity discounts are also available. On your letterhead, include information concerning the intended use of the books and the number of books you wish to purchase.

Visit us online at www.primapublishing.com

For my parents, Lutfee and Mariam Atieh;
my kids, Lutfee, Ramsey, Sami, and Tahani;
and Stephanie Atieh

Contents

Part One: Exploring Online Education

Part Two: Listing of Schools

Contents

Foreword

THE PUBLICATION OF a book on this topic—how to obtain a college degree via the Internet—suggests future opportunities nontraditional students have heretofore only dreamed about. Obtaining a college education from the convenience of your home, according to your own schedule, from an institution of your choosing, from anywhere in the world, portends a future that may one day be compared to the introduction of electricity in terms of its impact on students all over the world.

This book is particularly timely because it provides a succinct introduction to taking college courses on the Internet. By providing readers with a list of current colleges and universities that provide online classes, *How to Get a College Degree Via the Internet* can be a valuable starting point for students wishing to pursue this educational avenue. The book also warns readers about the importance of taking classes from an accredited institution and how to verify whether or not a school is really accredited.

The Internet has brought many exciting changes into our homes and offices that affect the way we do business and spend our leisure time. Now the Internet is bringing people all over the world the ability to take educational classes for college credit. *How to Get a College Degree Via the Internet* is a tool that can help you find a college or university degree program that is right for you.

DEAN L. HUBBARD
President, Northwest Missouri State University, Missouri

Acknowledgments

I DID NOT think writing a book would take so much effort, and I appreciate all the support from my friends and family in this exciting venture. I would like to thank Kathy Parrish and Scott Wells, Ed Colon, Don Tyes, Rabi Sahoo, and Cindy Nagel. Special thanks to Dr. David E. Stacey, Melody Lowe, Nancy Wilson, Dr. Nancy Thompson, Dr. Ahmad Atiyeh, and Jamie Miller from Prima Publishing, whose support made it possible for this book to come to life.

Introduction

WHEN I WAS working in Kuwait in the mid-1980s, I wanted to study for my master's degree in business without having to leave my job. I approached several universities in the United States and England with a proposal for an online higher education: I wanted a school to try transmitting lectures and tests through a modem. I even went as far as offering to fly to England from Kuwait every four months to take the exams. I had no luck with any of the five schools I approached. The dean of one prestigious British university concluded our two-hour meeting by saying; "You are wasting your time, young man. I really cannot see this happening now or in the future." Ironically, his university now offers courses over the Internet—only fifteen years later.

Everything new is looked upon with suspicion and caution and sometimes with rejection, and so it has been with the idea of using the Internet to pursue higher education. It is new, it is different, and it is unknown. It is natural to be cautious.

How would people from the mid-nineteenth century respond to the idea that in the future people would be able to fly across the ocean in a few hours? Or to talk to each other on the telephone across the world? I think their response would be no different than that of the British university dean.

When I started my research into online/distance learning, only forty schools offered this kind of education. Now it is offered by more than seventy schools, and this number is increasing by the month. I would not be surprised if, in the next five years, 50 percent of the 3,600 colleges and universities in the United States offered online education as an option. This is not such a surprising idea when you think back ten years: How many banks were offering automatic teller machines (ATMs) then? Online learning is a new paradigm of education whose time has come. Online education is not just an education, it is a whole new idea of learning. It is a cultural and technical revolution.

Getting a degree in higher education through online/distance learning may be a challenge, but *How to Get a College Degree Via the Internet* will make it easier for you to get started. This book provides the best and most current information possible from the learner's perspective about online education, and presents it in a format that is useful and easy to understand.

In Part I you'll learn about what online/distance learning is, how it works, and how you can integrate it into your life. You'll also learn some valuable tips about how to pick a school that meets your unique needs, how to finance your education, valuable Internet resources, and even how to find a job online. Part II offers an up-to-date listing of schools that currently offer online/distance learning, including curriculum and costs.

I hope this book broadens your basic knowledge of online/distance learning and introduces you to a new avenue of education you may have never thought possible.

Part One

Exploring Online Education

Higher Education Today

To be a "professional" in the contemporary job scene means initial and continuous training; to keep a job you will have to keep pursuing further knowledge and skills.

ADVANCES IN COMPUTER and communication technology affect all aspects of our lives—and education is no exception. The best and newest shift in education is the greatest change it has seen in a very long time: Both private and public sectors in international economies are undertaking huge efforts to build an online educational environment that is truly universally accessible. People who—because of time, money, and family constraints or physical disabilities—are unable to attend traditional colleges and universities can now take fuller advantage of higher education.

As our working world changes, so does education. The age of the average college student is older than it used to be. According to the National Center for Education Statistics, the enrollment of students under the age of twenty-five increased by only 2 percent between 1980 and 1990; in that same period, enrollment for older adults climbed 32 percent. More people of different ages means an increase in competition for seats in classrooms.

Some older students face further obstacles. Studying for a degree in the traditional manner demands a major time commitment.

Often it means travel away from family and employment. Traditional higher education cannot easily accommodate these students. For working professionals with family responsibilities, the pursuit of knowledge and training in the traditional manner is gradually becoming unattainable.

Higher education is also more important today than ever before. As national economies become integrated into new global markets, professional and career expectations are becoming more demanding. To have a career and excel at it, you must work hard to keep current with information technology:

- It is estimated that in the next ten years, 70 percent of the jobs available will be jobs that do not now exist— most of those jobs will be in information technology (IT).

- The US Department of Labor predicts that the IT field will account for 80 percent of all new jobs in the next decade.

- According to the Information Technology Association of America, there are already 350,000 jobs vacant in IT at large and mid-size US companies.

To be a "professional" in the contemporary job scene means keeping up to date; to keep a job you will have to keep pursuing further knowledge and skills. The new era is enforcing the old adage "You have to keep learning from cradle to rocking chair." Online/distance learning (online/DL) education allows busy people with full lives easier access to higher education and professional advancement. This means you: You can realize your full potential and achieve greater success in your life.

On the Internet, students can pursue an accredited degree program from a local college or a foreign university. Studying is still hard work, of course, just as it always has been. But now you can do this work from your home without having to abandon the rest of your life. The Internet abolishes distance, thus eliminating the substantial costs of giving up employment and the financial burden of international and local travel, accommodation, and living expenses.

OBSTACLES TO TRADITIONAL EDUCATION FOR NONTRADITIONAL STUDENTS

Until recently, traditional education was all there was: Students in their late teens and early twenties attended school and went on to the workplace. *Nontraditional students*—anyone outside of the eighteen- to twenty-five-year-old age range, including working and single mothers, women reentering education after raising a family, and working professionals—had to sacrifice a great deal of their everyday lives to pursue an accredited higher education. Some just gave up.

Not all that long ago, education was restricted to the rich. Universities were reserved for the training of a social elite, and working people could not manage its high cost. Postsecondary education for everyone is a modern achievement. With the improvement of the standard of living across the world in general and in the United States in particular, education became more affordable. Especially with the GI Bill after World War II, more people—at least, more men—in the United States could afford to attend colleges and universities. Women and minorities gradually began pursuing higher education in greater numbers as well.

During the last decade, however, the cost of education has begun to increase dramatically. Once again, education for everyone is threatened. If the cost of higher education continues to increase at such a rapid rate, at a time when more and more people want and need it, we could be returning to a traditional situation of exclusivity. If it costs too much to go to college, then the old situation will come around again, and higher education will again be only for the rich.

Direct Costs

The direct cost of education consists of tuition and fees, books, lab fees, and other expenses. These are increasing at a rapid rate. At the same time, the standard of living and discretionary income are increasing at a slower rate. In other words, the direct cost of education is rising too quickly for comfort, and more and more students must borrow money to attend college. This trend threatens to deprive the nation of the most important resource it has: educated and knowledgeable individuals.

Indirect Costs

The indirect cost of education is defined as any cost other than tuition, fees, and books. Consider the time you spend commuting to a college or a training location. Economists call this expense of time "opportunities forgone": All the things you could have been doing during that time—if you were not tied up in commuting to school—are opportunities forgone.

Now calculate how much money you could have earned if your schedule was more flexible. Add the price of public transportation to get to school, or the cost of gas, parking, insurance, and wear and tear on your car. Do not forget to take into account the cost of meals or snacks at school, clothing, child care, and the many other incidental expenses that are associated with going to college.

Compare these costs to the cost of staying at home or in the workplace to take your courses. This should give you an initial idea of the savings that distance learning can provide for you. If you extrapolate these savings over the time period required for you to get a degree, you will see that this represents a considerable amount of money.

Quality of Life Costs

Another important factor, albeit nonquantifiable, is the quality of your family and social life. Would you rather be commuting to school or spending time with your friends and loved ones?

Distance learning may hold a valuable key to your quality of life. For example, a professional woman making $30,000 a year decides to quit her job to get a graduate degree. During the eighteen months or two years it takes to complete her program, she will lose between $45,000 and $60,000 in wages earned. Her opportunity costs—it goes without saying—are prohibitively high. Many mothers and single parents are putting their education on hold because of the high cost of child care: How can you measure the opportunity costs here?

Course Availability

Most traditional schools cater to traditional students. Although many schools try to facilitate the needs of professionals and nontraditional students, their attempts are far from sufficient. A traditional curriculum adheres to a rigid structure. Traditional curricula are often time-honored and entrenched; they cannot escape their established routines and schedules. They have their customary arrangements and they are impervious to change. This or that course can only be offered in terms of available resources, with this or that professor, in this or that building using these or those facilities. With all these things in place, it is difficult to offer a course when the student needs to take it. In many cases, professional people have to wait as long as a year for a particular course to be offered at a convenient time at their local campus.

In this day and age, such a delay is starting to seem unnecessary. In the era of smart computers and high technology, the convenience of the institution should no longer triumph over the needs of the individual. It is true, of course, that all schools must operate as institutions; but one of the ways they must do so is by adapting to the fact that traditional and nontraditional students are two different markets with very different needs. It is almost

Photo by Bray Photography

**Dale Jungk,
business instructor**

I have a master of arts in English, but thought my work schedule would never give me the opportunity to pursue my doctorate degree—until I discovered [online education]. This new and exciting opportunity not only allows me to work on my Ph.D. around my schedule, but also saves me the burden of traveling. This means big savings, especially since the college of my choice is out of state.

impossible to target both markets with the same marketing tools and to serve both clients with the same educational methodologies.

Specialized Education

Perhaps the greatest obstacle to a traditional higher education has to do with specialty. Very often, professionals cannot find their desired field of study in the college or university closest to home. They must move to another city or to another country, incurring moving and traveling costs and all the attendant emotional sacrifices a person endures when leaving home.

Another great obstacle to specialization is the cost of running a university, which is quite high. As the need for higher education increases throughout the world, new universities are being founded in many different countries. Nevertheless, these institutions must compete nationally and internationally for highly paid experts in various fields. There is nothing easy about fostering and maintaining opportunities for specialization and expertise.

Conflict Between Business and Academia

The traditional conflict between academic and business culture is another kind of obstacle. The academic mind-set can isolate educational institutions from their everyday surroundings. This is often referred to as a historical hostility between "town and gown." One unfortunate result is that many institutions fail to integrate experts from business and industry into the educational process. Such out-of-date thinking only encourages this gap between the ways and means of traditional education and needs of people who must work for a living and who want to make a better life for themselves. Most traditional schools are still concerned mainly with traditional students.

Online education is designed to benefit people whose geographic location, work demands, physical or social conditions, personal circumstances, or family and community responsibilities impede their access to traditional university-level education. Fortunately, more and more schools are beginning to address the needs of nontraditional learners. And the good news is, their number is increasing.

2

Distance Learning and the Internet

The Internet is not a passing fad. It is the best opportunity for improving education since the mechanized printing presses of the early nineteenth century started putting books in the hands of millions of people.

THE UNITED STATES Distance Learning Association (USDLA) defines *distance learning* as "the delivery of education or training through electronically mediated instruction including satellite, video, audio graphic, computer, multimedia technology, and other forms of learning at a distance." In other words, when you are in one physical location and the teacher is in another, you have distance education.

THE HISTORY OF DISTANCE LEARNING

Online education is relatively new, but distance, or correspondence learning, has a long history. The granting of "external degrees" has existed for more than a century in Europe, Africa, and Asia. The Open University originated in the United Kingdom in 1971, growing out of Oxford University's version of continuing education, the WEA (Worker's Education Association), and other historically converging tendencies that pushed learning out beyond the walls of the university quadrangle. Today, the largest distance learning student body in the world is part of UNISA, the University of South Africa, with more than 200,000 people enrolled worldwide.

In the United States, universities have experimented with distance learning since the late nineteenth century. Columbia University began offering distance learning options in the 1920s. On the whole, however, distance learning remained relatively undeveloped throughout most of the twentieth century. Universities exclusively dedicated to distance learning began appearing in the United States in the early 1970s. Among the most notable pioneers are New York's Regents External Degree Program, now widely known as Regents College, and California's California Western University, now called California Coast University.

Because distance learning is not as fully developed yet in the United States as it will soon be, there is at present some feeling against distance learning degrees, even accredited ones. Some tradition-bound people regard distance learning to be a mark of an inferior education, and these degrees have been accepted in some occupations more than in others. Such preconceptions appear to be weakening as the viability of distance learning becomes more widely known and as such degree programs grow in number, size, and reputation.

According to a study released by the Department of Education, 33 percent of higher education institutions offered distance education to more than 700,000 students in 1995. And growth has escalated rapidly since then, according to Patrick Portway, founder of the U.S. Distance Learning Association in Livermore, California. The growth is so rapid that the Clinton administration, in response to the growing number of students seeking higher education via the Internet, is proposing to expand financial aid for distance learners.

The degree programs we have researched for this book are legitimate and reputable. You will not find here any programs where certification can be anything less than earned. In every case a distance learning program requires as much work of you as any other type of program. Indeed in some cases, distance learning programs require *more* work and study from their students than traditional programs!

DISTANCE LEARNING TODAY

Educational institutions usually rely on printed lecture material, although this is changing with the incursion of electronic media into the classroom and the ability of the computer to incorporate sound and images into teaching situations. Nonetheless, distance education still relies, for the most part, on the standard lecture. We can expect to see that change dramatically and soon, but, for the time being, distance learning implies a lecture that is printed on paper or recorded on video or audio tapes. Along with textbooks, these materials are mailed to students.

Often, as with the Open University in Great Britain, class materials are designed to accompany television programming. The student watches the lecture on television and then has a limited time to do the assignments and mail them back to the instructor to be graded. In most cases the communication is "asynchronous"—one person sends the materials, and the other person waits to receive them.

As stated earlier, many colleges and universities have been offering higher education programs through distance learning for some time. However, these programs are not always technologically sophisticated, nor do they cover all subjects. Traditionally, they cover mainly the humanities and very basic business courses. The process can be slow since it depends on regular mail service, or "snail mail." There are problems with televised learning schedules as well: Specific course programs are often broadcast at odd times so as not to compete with popular, money-making entertainment programs.

Perhaps the greatest shortcoming to date in distance education is the factor of technology: Either suitable technology simply has not been available or it has been too expensive to invest in. With the availability of powerful yet affordable personal computers and advanced communication technology, distance learning conducted online is now within the reach of most schools and students.

Today, distance learning means exciting new ways to learn, as technology makes the concept of "distance" much less important than it once was. You may watch a lecture broadcast via satellite by a university or an institution on the other side of the world. Or you may participate in a live session and communicate with your classmates and instructors through your home computer. And if you are too busy, you can have your computer download the live lecture while you are out or are sleeping at night, then you can watch the lecture at a later time.

WHAT IS THE INTERNET?

The *Internet*, or the *Net*, is a set of computers linked together over phone lines, fiber optic cables, satellite linkups, or other media. It is a vast and rapidly growing "network of networks," and in the very near future it will connect virtually every computer in the world with every other computer in the world.

You can earn your college degree over the Internet, but you can do much more:

- It allows you to keep in contact with your friends, classmates, and family around the world.

- It enables you to have access to hundreds of libraries to help you do your research.

- It is a goldmine of professional relationships where people in all fields share information about their work.

- It is a medium that offers unlimited business opportunities.

- It is a place where you can find a job or advertise for one, and soon you will be able to interview for that job on the Net. With the proper software and a camera, you can see the person you are talking to.

The number of people currently connected to the Internet is estimated to be 100 million, and this figure is growing at an astounding rate. It is a safe bet that soon most of the U.S. population will be online.

The Internet is not a passing fad. Quite simply, it is now the best opportunity for improving education since the mechanized printing presses of the early nineteenth century enabled the production of affordable books. The Internet began as part of a great military defense network, then became a research network, and then a communications network. College and university educators are just beginning to harness its mighty energies to the purposes of distance education.

The Internet is changing daily, which means that no one can provide an absolutely accurate list of sites and resources available. The good news is that the Internet itself provides tools for finding new resources or locating old ones. Infoseek, WebQuery, Yahoo!, Search.com, Lycos, and many other *search engines* that help you locate information by keywords or subjects are now freely available to Internet users. User costs may someday be attached to these services, but for the foreseeable future the Internet is free. And it is "free" in terms of more than money.

THE FREEDOM OF THE INTERNET

Freedom of expression thrives on the Internet. You can find anything here, from glorious love poetry to repulsive hate screeds.

Nancy C. Wilson, teacher

As a single parent, I received my bachelor's degree in the traditional manner. I worked two on-campus part-time jobs, went to classes all day, and did homework until 2 a.m. During that four years I lost contact with sleep and rest, but was well rewarded when I marched across the stage in cap and gown to receive my diploma.

I worked for two years when I remarried, had two more children, and stayed home for the next nine years as a full-time mom. I knew I needed to update my skills to reenter the teaching field and began to pursue my master's degree in education. This required traveling to a university forty-five miles away for night classes, driving snowy, treacherous roads, or spending six weeks attending summer school. After four years, I am still one class away from that elusive degree.

Now, after essentially twenty years as a full-time mom, I am back at work. At forty-six years of age, I have no accumulated retirement fund and am at the bottom of the pay scale.

Until [I learned about] online higher education, I hadn't given any thought to pursuing my doctorate degree. The travel, baby-sitters, cost, and inconvenience seem too much to bear. With online education, however, I not only see a viable option, but also a way to increase my earning power and future financial security.

This is the truly new, truly amazing thing about it: It connects everything to everything else. The works of Shakespeare could link to weather maps of the moon, which could link to today's *London Times* and tomorrow's weather maps of East McKeesport, Pennsylvania—and everything, everywhere, and everybody else in between.

Attempts to regulate the speech and conduct of people who use the Net have so far failed utterly. Many attempts to charge fees for services have also failed, quite spectacularly. For now, the Internet is the only easily accessed information source available to any person with the right equipment.

These factors of freedom, connectivity, and access add up to a really rather radical development in human culture and knowledge. Never in the history of humankind has getting information been easier. Educators and educational institutions are beginning to realize the potential of the Net. From kindergartens and grade schools to colleges and universities, schools are beginning to connect to each other in cyberspace. President Bill Clinton and Vice President Al Gore have supported various initiatives aimed at connecting every American classroom to the Internet. Most colleges and universities in the United States, Canada, and other countries now provide e-mail accounts to their students and faculty.

But there is much more to the Net beyond basic e-mail. On the World Wide Web, a "homepage" allows individuals, companies, and organizations of all kinds to provide information about themselves. Using full-color hypertext, graphics, and sound, people present themselves to the world with real excitement, creativity, and verve. With multiple user dimensions (MUDs), people from all over the world can construct an imagined space and then talk to one another in real time. The possibilities opened up by these various Net activities are widely acknowledged to be virtually limitless.

DISTANCE LEARNING MEETS THE INTERNET: INFINITE POSSIBILITY

The World Wide Web is probably the most significant recent development of the Internet. Some form or another of the Web, with its ability to provide various links to all other homepages on the Internet, will probably replace what we now know as television, the telephone, and the traditional correspondence and distance learning course.

Some colleges are already offering fully developed distance courses on the Internet. A very few are offering programs leading to a graduate degree earned totally on the Internet. The future of higher education is inextricably bound up with the development of the Internet, so much so that it is indeed safe to say that the use of the Internet for teaching and scholarship by both faculty and students will increase dramatically in the very near future.

If the Internet lives up to its promise and blossoms into the truly revolutionary, truly worldwide network of connected computers that it looks like it is going to be, then we will have to begin thinking in new ways about our old world. Old constraints of time and space are not relevant on the Internet. In Net time Japan is as close to you as your computer, New York is no nearer or farther than Beijing, and snow, sleet, and dark of night are truly vanquished as the worst enemies of the timely post.

E-mail flies out to its destinations in milliseconds. Letters that take a week to cross the ocean to Europe from North America now arrive in minutes. Huge files can be downloaded and duplicated and dispersed across the commercial universe in seconds. In the business world, people use e-mail to avoid telephone tag. In the world of academia, instructors use e-mail to consult with the entire class by sending a message to everyone at once on a *listserv*, or they tutor individual pupils in a cyberspace "study" built for the purpose of the one-on-one conference at an electronic university.

Already the market in educational software is flooded with multimedia and teleconferencing software that can simulate the teaching processes of a traditional learning situation. The Internet brings a new dimension to education: the ability to share information with other students not only across campus, but across the world.

Another very exciting feature of this new multidimension is the access students will have to hundreds, even thousands, of libraries now or soon to be online, as well as the creation of new kinds of electronic archives for research and scholarship. The searching, sorting, and retrieval capacities of data-banked libraries are absolutely unprecedented, as are the many other possibilities for a new, highly interactive kind of study. Scholarship is energized by the Internet and its wholly new ways of reading, writing, and researching.

Unlimited Resources

Like the worldwide library that it is, the Internet encourages students and teachers to find and use new information. New Internet search tools with highly developed, elaborately personalized sorting abilities will soon be available. These will allow individuals to find, retrieve, and tentatively organize the most recent, interesting, or relevant information, data, images, and even software that they desire.

In traditional institutions of higher learning, students often do not interact with fellow students beyond the walls of the classroom they share at appointed times. On the Internet, students have the opportunity to interact with other students around the world. Instructors have similar opportunities to interact with other instructors teaching the same subject, anywhere in the world. Instructors can also invite comments and ideas from experts at other universities and in industry, regardless of their geographical location. If, for instance, a teacher or student has a problem with something stated by the writer of the course textbook, there is nothing to stop that student or teacher from sending a question, comment, or criticism to the textbook author at his or her e-mail address or homepage.

Saving Money, Time, and the Environment

Because information changes so quickly and the process of researching, writing, and publishing is so slow, it is almost impossible for any textbook to be current by the time it reaches the market. Internet technology provides an inexpensive way for information to be updated and distributed instantly so that students and teachers always have access to current information.

Using the Internet can also save time. Students have access to the libraries of the world in their own home office. With no need to leave the house to search the stacks or to request material to be sent to them from around the world, they can accomplish their work much faster.

It is to be hoped that many corporations will encourage their employees to pursue higher education and training via the Internet. Because Internet education need not involve an employee's protracted absence from work, both the employer's and the employee's costs are minimized. Everyone benefits.

Finally, the Internet also means environmental savings. Textbooks are printed on paper—a renewable resource, but not an unlimited one. Traditional print is part of a system that relies on industrial technology that destroys natural resources. Online publishing will save tremendous amounts of paper and therefore tremendous numbers of trees.

The Internet Does Not Discriminate

Electronic communities are real communities, and problems that plague the real world also affect the virtual world of the Internet. On earth, there are no perfect worlds. However, physical differences need not affect communication on the Internet the way they too often do in face-to-face communication. The Internet does not discriminate. Socially induced prejudices toward appearance, gender, race, country of origin, and behaviors are virtually eliminated on the Net. Here, students are judged solely on their performance.

Simplicity

The Internet is a powerful tool that is relatively simple to use. Finding and retrieving information is a matter of learning to use search engines, and good minds are hard at work researching and developing these devices so that they are easy for everyone to use.

The Internet makes technicians of us all; we have to know the basics of the software and hardware. Certain skills have to be mastered: You have to transform your typing skills into "keyboarding," and you have to understand that a "mouse" isn't a furry little animal scurrying about your cupboards. But even though this very basic technical know-how is a must, participating in an online degree program does not require advanced computer skills.

A Global Classroom

Precisely because the hypertextual nature of the Internet plays upon an innate human desire to connect this with that, and that with this, and then these with everything else, you won't find the world of the World Wide Web an inhospitable environment. It is a warm, not a cold place to be.

Surf among the thousands upon thousands of individual homepages already out there on the Net and you will find people rejoicing in all the color and sound and fun of self-discovery and expression. The inviting feel of the thing accounts for the fact that the Internet has the capacity to be the largest educational enterprise ever undertaken.

It can even be said that since such a large cross-section of life is represented online(or will be soon), the Net is an education in and onto itself. While much of what we have learned has come from formal educational situations in traditional schools, every individual person is capable of learning to learn, so to speak, on the Internet. We can learn more than we ever dreamed we could know about ourselves and our world from self-planned and self-directed learning activities.

Because online education offers a variety of learning environments, the experience can be very rich. You can learn from and interact with not only your instructor, but also with other students. You are no longer restricted to the limited experience of one individual and the learning environment of few classmates. The world is your classroom.

3

Is Online Education Right for You?

Online education provides learning environments that literally did not exist before.

MOST PEOPLE AGREE that having a college or university degree enables you to earn a higher wage than someone without a degree. Simply put, a degree helps you attain a higher quality of life. However, it's not always so easy to go back to school to earn a degree—there are bills to pay, a family to support, and long hours at the office.

Thankfully, recent advances in technology and the rise of the Internet are beginning to make education more convenient and less expensive for all kinds of students, especially nontraditional students. If you feel that you cannot afford to leave your job or family to study full-time, online/distance learning (online/DL) may be just what you are looking for.

TRADITIONAL AND NONTRADITIONAL STUDENTS

The popular image of the "student" is deeply woven into the fabric of North American culture by such writers as F. Scott Fitzgerald and movies such as *Animal House.* Stereotypically, these eternal undergraduates are carefree hedonists who can afford the time and the money it takes to have four years of campus fun. In reality, they are simply the people around and for whom the present system of higher education has been built. They are the young people dormitories are built to house. They fill lecture halls and cafeterias and student unions. They live and work "on campus."

But there is a large population of nontraditional students— men and women over the age of twenty-five—who are not served by this traditional setup. These people, also called "adult learners" or "lifetime learners," are a relatively new phenomenon. Unlike traditional students, they are quite diverse in their lives and needs. Online learning provides an excellent opportunity, and sometimes the only opportunity, for these people to obtain their education.

ARE YOU A GOOD CANDIDATE FOR ONLINE EDUCATION?

Online/DL is particularly suited to people who are unable to attend classes regularly due to work, family, or other obligations. Here are just a few of the categories that can benefit.

Professionals

Professional men and women who have already started a career are working full time to keep that career. Add to this the responsibilities that come with supporting a family, and you have a person with little time to allocate for education.

Contemporary professionals seem to live on the go. Microwave ovens were invented for them, as were the edge-city motels and extended-stay apartments that rise high alongside the perimeters of urban airports. Their jobs require frequent travel within the country or abroad. The modem attached to the laptop or notebook computer is changing their lives in many ways, not

Ashraf T. Madoukh, President, Computer Consulting Group (CCG)

I had to put pursuing my graduate study on hold for the last three years because my work as a computer consultant for small and large corporations keeps me so busy. After a long day at work, I like to spend the little time left out of the day with my wife and children.

I believe that without online education, I would never have been able to start graduate school. I can now study from my home office while enjoying the company of my family.

the least of which is the possibility of continuing a formal education online.

Single Parents

Single parents are in a special position. They must work to support their children. Most cannot leave their jobs to go to school full time, and even going part time means finding and paying for child care. Online/DL allows these parents to study in their own home, in their own time, nearly eliminating the need for child care and more time away from home.

Physically Challenged

Physically challenged individuals who are not comfortable in classroom settings or who are unable to drive to school can benefit from online/DL classes. They can study in the comfort of their own home without having to worry whether or not the school can make adjustments for their special needs.

Educators

Educators are responsible for educating others. They cannot skip many school days to further their own education. Online education allows teachers to pursue new avenues of interest and acquire specialized and postgraduate degrees.

International Professionals

International professionals and students who want or need certain specializations, or who simply enjoy cosmopolitan boundary-crossing, may want to work "here" but live "there." Online education makes it possible to study in North America from abroad or vice versa. Degrees awarded by accredited American colleges and universities are highly valued and recognized around the world. International professionals and students can now get a US or Canadian college degree without leaving home.

Military Personnel

Military personnel are often stationed in isolated or remote areas. Even if they are near an urban center, their duty schedule usually does not allow them the freedom to attend traditional universities. For them, online education is a boon.

QUESTIONS AND ANSWERS ABOUT ONLINE LEARNING

Having read this far, you may be thinking that online learning is perfect for you. However, you may also be wondering how certain aspects of it work. Below are some commonly asked questions and their answers. Some topics are covered in more detail in other chapters.

Q. Are online degrees legitimate?

Yes, degrees offered online through a regionally accredited college, or through institutions that are accredited by any agency recognized by the US Department of Education, are legitimate. State-approved college degrees are not accredited, but can be of good value, especially degrees offered by colleges in California. California has strong requirements on state-approved colleges.

There are, of course, "fly by night" businesses that will print diplomas for a price. The granting of phony degrees in exchange for money has been with us for about as long as legitimate schools have existed, and the virtual world of the Internet is bound to bring out more than a few old wolves dressed in new sheep's clothing.

Q. Will my degree say *online* on it?

No, your online degree is the same as an on-campus degree. It has the same title and value.

Q. Is online education easier than traditional education?

Not necessarily. Most online programs are designed by the same teachers who designed traditional programs, and they have the same academic requirements. Online study is only easier in that it is more convenient for the student.

Q. Does getting an online degree take less time than a traditional degree?

To some degree the answer is yes, because you don't have to wait a semester or a year for a course to be offered. Here are some general timelines: associate degree, eighteen months to two years; bachelor's degree, three to four years; master's degree, eighteen months to two years; doctoral degree, three years or more. Some people finish their degrees online in less time.

Donald R. Tyes, private business consultant and special enforcement officer

Some years ago, I was a senior university student when I was offered a promising career opportunity. I took the offer with the intention that I would complete my education after training for my new job, but I was sadly mistaken. Once this job began, there was no time for me to fit college classes into my schedule.

It took me nine years to build up enough seniority in my job so that I could arrange my schedule to complete my undergraduate degree. By that time I had a wife and two children who were also competing for my time, in addition to the hours I spent at work preparing for classes. Had online education been available then, I could have completed my education at my convenience and in a more timely fashion.

When I decided to go to graduate school a couple of years later, I ran into the same obstacles—time, scheduling, and work. With some creative scheduling and a lot of personal sacrifices, I finally completed my MBA. Again, had online education been available, I undoubtedly would have pursued that alternative.

With the convenience and increasing availability of online education, career-minded professionals and those who have forgone their education because of work will no longer have to chose their jobs over their education or vice-versa. Now they can have both.

Q. Is online education less expensive than traditional education?

> It is if you take into consideration that you are saving the cost of campus living expenses or transportation expenses to get to and from school. Online credit hour cost is the same as the cost of a credit hour on campus in most colleges; few colleges charge less.

Q. How do I take my exams?

> Most schools use proctors in many states and in some foreign countries. If your state does not have a proctor, you can recommend one to your school. The proctor will monitor your exam to make sure you stay within the prescribed time limit and meet the school's standards.

Q. How much time should you allocate to studying for an online program?

> The answer to this question is rather difficult; it depends on the program, your academic background, and your experience. Generally, you should budget at least ten hours a week for studying.

Q. Do online programs offer financial aid?

> Regionally accredited colleges and universities participate in the federal financial aid program, and many of them offer financial aid for qualified applicants. State-approved colleges cannot offer financial aid through the federal program, although most offer an installment payment plan. In many cases, employers reimburse the cost of your education.

Q. Do I have to be computer savvy to enroll in an online program?

> No, you need basic computer skills only. Some schools offer free training for a week or two on the Internet before you start your program.

Q. Are all fields of study available online?

> No. Many colleges and universities are not yet offering online education, but the number is increasing and the technology is improving. The next few years will witness a dramatic increase in number of institutions offering this kind of education and hence in the variety of degrees available.

Q. Can I study from a foreign country?

> Yes, you can be anywhere on the planet that offers computer access. If you have a place to plug in your computer and a telephone, you can do your online study.

4

What You'll Need: Equipment and Skills

There are many reasons to have a computer. One of the best is to pursue a college degree.

IN ORDER TO make use of the innovative technology that will get you started studying online for an undergraduate or advanced degree, you need to have a computer and access to the Internet.

When the school admits you to its online/DL program, it will provide you with a user ID and a password to enable you to access the school's programs. In many schools your tuition pays for full access to the Internet.

Even if you have Internet access through your employer, for the purpose of online/DL learning, you should also have access in your home. This will allow you to learn on your own time and not antagonize your employer. This means you will need some basic services, hardware, and software.

INTERNET SERVICE PROVIDERS

To get on the Internet, you will need to sign up with an Internet service provider (ISP). An ISP is a business entity that sells Internet access to the public, in the same way your phone company sells you phone service. There are many national and local ISPs to choose from, including MCI, NetCom, AT&T, Sprint, America Online, Microsoft Network, and CompuServe, among others. Most national providers have toll-free numbers, which you can find by calling the toll-free information operator at 1-800-555-1212. Local ISPs may be as close as your home town. You are given a local phone number to dial, so you are not charged for using the phone. Most communities have a growing number of providers—look in the Yellow Pages of your phone book, or talk to friends and ask who they use.

Here are some tips for selecting an ISP:

- Select the ISP that provides you with unlimited access for a flat fee (does not charge you by the hour). Average monthly charges are currently $15 to $20, with no additional charges.

- If you travel a lot, and you want to stay online, you are better off with a national provider.

- Make sure that the national provider you choose has a toll-free number to access and that there are no phone charges for using it. Even three cents a minute can add up to a lot of money.

- Your ISP should not only provide you with Internet access, but with technical support as well. If you have a question, don't hesitate to e-mail or call your Internet service provider.

HARDWARE

If you do not have a computer at home, going online will require you to buy one with certain features. At minimum, you will need a computer and monitor, a modem, and a printer.

Computer

The computer you use for your online education doesn't have to be very fast or have a lot of memory. A 486 machine with 8MB of RAM can do the job. But if you would like to take full advantage of the online features, I recommend the following configuration:

- 166 to 330MHz Pentium processor (the faster the better)
- 16 to 32MB of RAM (memory)
- 14- to 17-inch high-resolution monitor
- 2 to 4MB of video memory
- 512KB of cache
- sound card, speakers, and a microphone
- 12 to 24X CD-ROM drive
- 2.0 to 4.0GB hard drive

At the time of publication, such a configuration ranges in price between $1,200 and $2,000.

If your job requires a lot of travel, you might want to consider a laptop. Laptops are slightly more expensive than desktop computers, but they provide a convenient way to access the Internet from virtually any location. A configuration similar to the one above currently ranges in price from $1,400 to $2,400.

Modem

A modem is a very important piece of equipment in this technology. The higher the speed of your modem, the faster (and cheaper) you can send and receive information. Again, a 33.6K modem can do the job, but a 56K modem is much better. Most new computers come with a suitable modem built in. If you don't have a fast modem in your computer, get an external modem. The price range varies, and it is going down by the month. Currently, you can purchase a fast modem for about $100.

Netiquette

The Internet is a vastly populated place, and Netiquette (Internet etiquette) outlines a set of "manners" or "rules of the road" to help keep things civilized. Because communicating via the Internet usually lacks a personal interface, it is imperative that you understand the virtual social mores so you don't inadvertantly offend someone.

For example, when you write an e-mail message, don't "shout." WRITING IN ALL CAPITAL LETTERS, LIKE THIS, is perceived as shouting. Another good point is to never assume that a message you write will be completely private. Even if you delete it, the message may be stored somewhere else, and it could come back to haunt you. To be safe, never write anything that you may later regret. There are many other guidelines to know and follow, and an excellent Web site to visit for more information is *http://www.albion.com/netiquette/index.html.*

A related site offers a warm welcome and practical advice for "newbies"—new Internet users who are still learning the Internet ropes. To avoid the pitfalls many new users encounter, check out the site *http://www.newbiesguide.com.*

If you really crave speed on the Internet, there is a nice device available now on the market. A satellite dish, similar to a TV dish, can allow you to get on the Internet with a speed of 400K—that is, more than ten times the speed of 33.6K modem. This technology means you can actually download a movie over the Internet in a few minutes. The price currently ranges from $250 to $300. If you select the dish, check with your Internet provider first to see if it supports this technology. The monthly cost could range from $60 to $120 depending on when and how many hours you use the Internet.

Printer

A printer allows you to print your documents and assignments. Currently, you can purchase a new printer that will do everything you need it to do for $200 to $300.

PC Digital Video Camera

A digital video camera supports your video-conferencing needs and provides the convenience of face-to-face communications from your desktop or notebook PC. This way your instructor, classmates, friends, and family will be able to see an image of you on their computer screens. (Don't worry, others can see you only if you want them to—you can always turn the camera off.) If the people at the other end of the connection are also camera-equipped, you can see a picture of them on your monitor. A color digital camera costs between $200 and $300; a black and white one costs about $100.

SOFTWARE

Windows 95 is the most common platform currently being used on microcomputers. This state-of-the-art software comes already installed on most computers. Although this book is geared toward PC users, Macintosh users will not have any problems taking advantage of online education. Check with your Mac vendor for appropriate configurations.

A word processing package such as Microsoft Word or Word-Perfect should be installed on your system. Most of your communication with the school will involve word processing. My favorite software package is Microsoft Office 97, which includes very helpful programs such as Word for word processing, Power-Point for designing presentations, Access for designing data-bases, and Excel for creating spreadsheets.

Optional Software

Other software packages can ease the online study process.

- Voice E-Mail: This software package allows you to record a voice message and send it as an e-mail, saving you from typing everything. It costs about $29. A free Voice E-Mail player is available so that people can listen to the Voice E-Mail messages you send them even if they don't have Voice E-Mail. More information is available at: *http://www.bonzi.com.*

- ViaVoice Gold: This speech-recognition software allows you to train your computer to recognize your voice so you can speak to your machine rather than type. For slow typists, this can be a lifesaver. It works with most common word processing packages. For more informa-tion, check *http://www.ibm.com/viavoice.* The software costs around $149.

- WebPhone: WebPhone, a telephone software package that provides real-time voice communications, allows you to talk to other people who have the same software, without incurring long-distance telephone bills. The only costs will result from your Internet Service Provider's standard Internet connection rates. To use WebPhone, you need an Internet connection, microphone, and speakers. You can get more information and download a free trial version of WebPhone by accessing *http://connect.netspeak.com* and then clicking on WebPhone 3.1.

The Ten Commandments for Computer Ethics from the Computer Ethics Institute

1. Thou shalt not use a computer to harm other people.
2. Thou shalt not interfere with other people's computer work.
3. Thou shalt not snoop around in other people's files.
4. Thou shalt not use a computer to steal.
5. Thou shalt not use a computer to bear false witness.
6. Thou shalt not use or copy software for which you have not paid.
7. Thou shalt not use other people's computer resources without authorization.
8. Thou shalt not appropriate other people's intellectual output.
9. Thou shalt think about the social consequences of the program you write.
10. Thou shalt use a computer in ways that show consideration and respect.

Excerpted from *The Net:User Guidelines and Netiquette* by Arlene Rinaldi. *http://www.fau.edu/rinaldi/net/ten.html*

Browser

You will also need a browser: a program that enables you to access the World Wide Web and use the Internet. The most common browsers on the market are Netscape Navigator and Microsoft Internet Explorer. Both are available on the Net and can be downloaded free of charge.

Microsoft Internet Explorer can be found at: *http://www.microsoft.com*. Netscape Navigator can be found at: *http://www.netscape.com/download*.

Antivirus Software

Computer viruses are "digital infections" created by malicious programmers. Viruses cause unwanted behavior on a computer and range from being relatively harmless to very destructive.

Computer viruses do *not* infect humans! On the other hand, they do behave like a biological virus: They can replicate themselves and spread from one computer to another when you use an infected disk or download an infected file.

There are some measures you can use to protect your computer from being infected by viruses. To learn more about them and how to practice safe computing, visit this site: *http://galaxy.einet.net:80/galaxy/Engineering-and-Technology/Computer-Technology/Security/david-hull/galaxy.htm*.

You can also install virus-finding-and-eradicating software on your computer to warn you if you are infected. Check your local software store to find the latest versions, and upgrade as often as possible with free downloads over the Internet.

SKILLS

You don't have to be a computer guru to study online, but you need to have some basic knowledge of how to use your computer and navigate the Internet. You can accomplish that by attending some introductory courses to computers in your local community. Your Internet provider may also be a valuable source of training, or you can get a friend to give you a few hours of computer tutoring. There are also a number of books and videos that explain the basics simply and clearly.

Most of your communication will be through the keyboard, so it will save you a lot of time and frustration to be able to type. You don't have to type eighty words a minute—or even forty words a minute—just enough to be able to find the keys on the keyboard. *Typing Tutor* and other software packages can teach you how to type relatively quickly and painlessly.

SPECIAL CONSIDERATIONS FOR INTERNATIONAL STUDENTS

If you live in a country where Internet access is very new and not easily available, your access to the Internet does not have to be online. It can be "batch." With such a setup, you do not receive messages immediately, but after an interlude, such as an hour or a day. You will still be able to do most of your college work successfully.

If Internet access is not available at your house, find an Internet "cafe." These cyberspace gathering places are becoming popular in many countries. Internet cafes have many computers available to the public, which they allow you to use for a monthly fee or hourly rate. Some libraries also have public Internet access.

ONLINE COURSES: STRUCTURE AND DELIVERY

Studying online is a new experience for everyone, but in some ways it's not so different from attending a lecture in a classroom. Once you connect to the college system via the World Wide Web, using your user name and ID, you might find messages from your instructor or your classmates in your personal mailbox or in the class forum. The class forum is like your classroom. It is where you will share and discuss information with the class. Let's take a closer look at how it works.

Program Delivery

Schools vary in their delivery methods, but most schools should provide you with the following:

- a structured World Wide Web environment

- bulletin boards for discussion

- Internet chat facilities (chat rooms)

- e-mail

Most schools use an asynchronous mode of communication, which does not require you to be on your computer at any specific time. Some schools use a synchronous (real-time) mode of communication. Although this method transfers the real learning experience to the student live, especially when equipped with a video camera, it is restricting. You have to be at the computer at certain times. This may be inconvenient, especially if you live in a different time zone than your instructor.

The best scenario would be for schools to offer synchronous (live) lectures as well as having the lectures stored on videotapes or CDs, which could then be mailed to students to review at their convenience. This would allow the educational experience to be transferred to all kinds of students.

Course Material

Most schools still use the traditional, hard copy textbook combined with study questions and exercises in their online courses. Other colleges use videotapes as their main delivery tool of course material. They tape every lecture and send you the tapes for the full week. Other schools will have the study material of the course you are taking on their Web site, which you can access at any time.

Assignments

Usually, assignments include reading or watching the lecture material and answering the associated questions. The exercises vary according to the program you are taking. A typical assignment for a computer programming course would be to write a computer program or create a database and e-mail it to your instructor for evaluation.

Exams

Tests and exams may be handled in two different ways. Some schools might ask you to assign a proctor to supervise your exam. A proctor is usually somebody who works in a college, a library, or any other institution. The proctor has to be approved by the college. The test material is sent directly to the proctor; His or her role is to assure the integrity of the examination process by verifying your identity and monitoring the time limit allocated to the exam. The cost of proctoring is usually paid by the student.

Other colleges might allow you to take the test on your computer and send the answers within a certain time frame. Still other schools might replace the exam with a project.

Chat Rooms

The course you are taking might have a chat room, a place where you can communicate with other people in a "virtual room" on the Internet. This is a way for you to chat to and exchange ideas with your fellow classmates as a group and in real time.

E-mail

E-mail is the way you communicate with your instructor or another student privately. You can send messages to your instructor or ask for explanations. It works better than a phone because you don't have to play phone tag or wait until a certain hour of the day to call. E-mail has proven to be a very reliable medium of communication, and it is basically free. You can get a free e-mail account from the following Web site: *http://www.hotmail.com.*

Many schools also have a virtual "bulletin board" for each course. This is a place on the Net where students can post

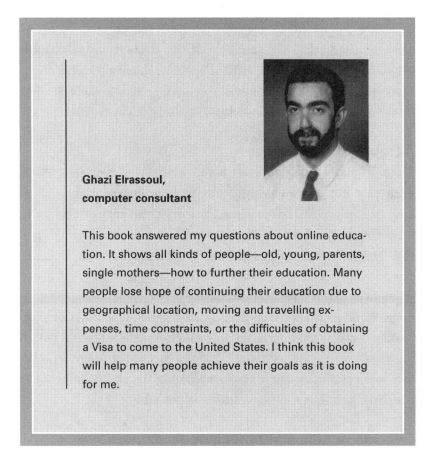

Ghazi Elrassoul, computer consultant

This book answered my questions about online education. It shows all kinds of people—old, young, parents, single mothers—how to further their education. Many people lose hope of continuing their education due to geographical location, moving and travelling expenses, time constraints, or the difficulties of obtaining a Visa to come to the United States. I think this book will help many people achieve their goals as it is doing for me.

questions by e-mail for everybody taking the course to read and respond to.

STUDYING AT HOME

Taking a course online may sound to some people like an easier way to study, merely because it is a more convenient way to study. However, don't be fooled into thinking that online courses take less effort! Online courses and programs offered by accredited colleges usually are designed by the same instructors who designed the traditional programs. They are not any "easier" than any other kind of academic work. Intellectual work is real work—hard work. Even though you can study from the comfort of your home, you will need to allocate as much time and attention as possible to each course you take. The following suggestions will help you create an effective study environment.

A Room of One's Own

Create a study space in your home where you can set up your computer and where you can study without interruption, such as a spare bedroom. If you want to deduct the cost of the space from your taxes, the IRS likes you to have doors on the room you read and write in (check with your accountant for more details).

Dress for Success

Some students dress for their online/DL session as they would do if they were attending a regular classroom or even an actual business meeting. This doesn't mean you need to wear a power suit to work online from your own home, but you should treat your study time more than a little bit formally.

Consider a Second Phone Line

A phone line dedicated to the Internet is not absolutely necessary but it can be very helpful. If you want friends to be able call you or your family while you are online with the school, you should definitely consider adding a second line. Most phone companies will provide a basic phone line, with no additional features, for $12 to $15 a month. This line should not have "call waiting": Call waiting can break your Internet connection, causing your files to be damaged.

Manage Your Time

Get into the habit of studying at certain times of the day or evening. Assume the discipline to establish boundaries around educational work in your home, and ask your family members to respect those boundaries. This will probably take some adjusting on all sides. Let good will and patience rule the day.

Think of each study session as a business meeting: It should have a starting and an ending time. In the same way, think of schoolwork as part of a job—give yourself deadlines and stick to them. Finally, use your time well by being convinced of its value.

Develop the Ability to Concentrate

Concentration is a real skill, especially at the end of a busy day, and you may have to prepare carefully for it. Don't be too concerned if it takes a while to focus your mind on schoolwork; like any skill, you will need to practice it. You will get better at it. Unlike many other life skills, however, the concentration you need in order to do academic work can elude you if you try too hard. Try to be Zen-like about it: Don't rush at it or try to grab it. Never panic if it doesn't come to you. Like any other personal activity, you must find what works for you. "Study to be Quiet," is the British saying. What do you need to do so that you are relaxed but alert?

When you sit down to a work session, close your eyes and concentrate on slowing down the busyness of the day. Breathe easy. Be quiet. Read something short and simple to focus your eyes on words. Imagine your pulse calming, your blood slowing, and your heartbeat steady and strong. Clear the mind. Begin.

5

How to Choose a School

Take your time in reviewing and verifying information about the school you choose: The length of time and the money you will end up spending in obtaining your degree justify your cautious and detailed investigation.

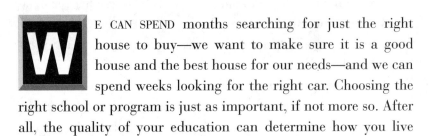E CAN SPEND months searching for just the right house to buy—we want to make sure it is a good house and the best house for our needs—and we can spend weeks looking for the right car. Choosing the right school or program is just as important, if not more so. After all, the quality of your education can determine how you live and work for the rest of your life.

HOW TO CHOOSE A SCHOOL

Read the list of schools in Part II carefully. Select five to ten schools that seem to suit your needs according to the program they offer, the cost, and so on. Then follow these steps:

1. Visit the Web sites of schools you have selected, and see what they have to say.

2. Send each school that interests you an e-mail message requesting information about your area of study. Many sites on the Web have links to electronic mailers, which means that you will be able to send a message of inquiry from the homepage of the site to the school. Remember: Always ask for all of the information an institution can send you, including admissions forms and information about financial aid.

3. Review the catalogs you received.

4. Verify the school's accreditation status by calling the US Department of Education (USDOE) at (202) 708-7417. If you would like to know more about accreditation, you can visit the USDOE online at *http://www.ed.gov/* or at *http://www.ed.gov/offices/OPE/pubs/Accred/part1.html.*

5. Check the Better Business Bureau in the area near the proposed school and ask for a full report on the school.

6. Ask if the school can provide names of alumni to whom you can talk about the program and school.

7. Check with your employer about the possibility of tuition reimbursement and the potential of a promotion when you obtain the degree.

8. Check the residency requirements of the school. Find out whether the school requires any residence periods for the program, or if the degree can be obtained totally online.

9. Ask the school if it has an assurance plan for students. You may be able to obtain a document in writing guaranteeing that the cost will not rise while you are attending the college.

10. Verify the cost per semester or quarter credit hour and find out if the school charges higher tuition for out-of-state students (even though you will be online).

11. Check the availability of courses and instructors. What intervals are classes taught in? Will you have to wait for a course to be offered again if it has been offered recently? This is a special concern if enrollment is not large in the institution or in the program.

12. Make a plan. If it is a small school or program, find out what courses are offered when, and when you will be able to take specific courses. Estimate the length of your program; if you are studying for an associate degree, plan for two years; for a bachelor's degree, plan for four years; for a master's degree, plan for two or three years; for a Ph.D., plan for four to six years. Put this plan together and show it to an advisor or the department chairperson. Make it more than a suggested outline by putting it in writing. See if you can get someone in authority in your program to sign off on it.

13. Check the overall population of the school and of the program you are interested in. Does this college truly cater to online students? What sources of assistance are available? Does the program maintain chat sessions or listserv discussion groups for its off-campus students? Are you offered full Internet access? Can you use interlibrary loan? Can you get counseling, of whatever kind, if you need it?

14. Complete the financial aid application to see how much assistance you qualify for.

15. Find out the names of the instructors who will be teaching your courses. How active is each in his or her respective profession? Have they published books or articles? Have they been teaching for a long time? Have they won any awards for teaching or community service? Send them e-mail notes. Ask them questions about their

Tressa Lucas-Grayson, marketing and management student

Online education provides me with the opportunity to pursue degrees that I had not thought possible due to time constraints and other factors. With the help of this book, I have taken the necessary steps to achieve my goal of acquiring my master's degree, and eventually my doctorate degree. Most importantly, I don't have to sacrifice my family or my job in my pursuit of excellence.

courses and professional specialties. Get to know them before you start working with them.

16. Most schools charge fees in addition to tuition. Those extra charges can add up a substantial amount of money. Try to get a written estimate of the total cost of your program.

These steps are a suggested plan of action. Feel free to use any additional techniques to verify the quality of your education. Some schools are starting to offer one or two weeks of free trial online courses. This offers you an excellent opportunity to see how a program functions—take advantage of it.

Once you have all the information you need, take your time in reviewing and verifying it. The length of time and the money you will end up spending in obtaining your degree justifies a cautious and detailed investigation. Just because a university is well-known does not mean it will have a convenient and suitable program for you. By the same token, a small or little-known college may be able to provide you with the quality education you need. Once you have answers you are satisfied with, submit the required documents to the admissions office.

ACCREDITATION

Although regional accreditation provides online/DL students with the assurance that certain quality standards have been met, many high-quality distance learning universities opt not to go through the complex and expensive accreditation process. So how do you determine the quality of such a school?

Regional Accreditation

Accreditation is a complex and lengthy process. In most countries, national governments either run universities or license them. The most notable exception to this is the United States. The United States has a two-tiered system: State and private universities are accredited by regional agencies; some universities are approved by the state in which a school is located.

For purposes of higher education accreditation, the United States is divided into six regions. Accreditation in each of theses regions is provided by separate regional accrediting associations. The six regional associations are recognized by the United States Department of Education (USDOE) and the Council on Post-secondary Accreditation. Accreditation of an institution is awarded only after a rigorous evaluation by a regional accrediting team. Each team is composed of senior academic administrators from accredited colleges and universities operating in the same region as the institution seeking accreditation. Reciprocity agreements among the six regional associations allow a university accredited by one agency to operate in other regions as an accredited institution.

Each school undergoes a comprehensive evaluation process to ensure that the degree programs offered by regionally accredited institutions maintain consistently high quality, regardless of geographical location. Schools that are accepted can be counted on to offer quality programs that are accredited within the United States and abroad.

Regional Accrediting Bodies

Even though regional accreditation is a voluntary and non-governmental process, it is widely regarded as quasi-mandatory, as an authoritative indication of quality. The following regional accrediting bodies are recognized by the US Department of Education:

- Middle States Association of Colleges and Schools (MSACHE)
- New England Association of Schools and Colleges (NEASC)
- North Central Association of Colleges and Secondary Schools (NCACS)
- Northwest Association of Schools and Colleges (NWASC)
- Southern Association of Colleges and Schools (SACS)
- Western Association of Schools and Colleges (WASC)

A number of new accrediting groups with genuine standards are currently seeking USDOE recognition. Until they do achieve such recognition, they can approve colleges and universities

Beware of Diploma Mills

Beware the "diploma mill" that uses a well-known name in order to deceive potential students. Foreign students may be particularly vulnerable to these deceptive practices.

- **False State School**: A name containing the word "State" such as "XYZ State University," usually implies it is an accredited state institution. In the United States you can name an institution a state institution and not be accredited by any of the accrediting agencies recognized by the USDOE. Always verify the accreditation.

- **Deceptive School Names**: Do not assume the name of the school is the name you think it is. "Harward" is not the same as "Harvard," and "MET" is not the same as "MIT." Names such as National or International don't mean that they carry any regional accreditation.

- **False Advertising**: On the World Wide Web, any institution can make itself look very impressive and real. Just because a school has a well-designed homepage does not mean it is a legitimate institution. If you don't know the school, go beyond its Web site and investigate it thoroughly.

- **Nonaccredited Programs**: Just because the school is regionally accredited, that does not mean all its programs are accredited. In many cases, an accredited school will have all its programs accredited. But some programs might be under development or in the process of accreditation, or simply don't meet the accreditation guidelines.

according to their own standards, but they cannot claim to be accrediting bodies recognized by the US Department of Education.

Other Valid Accreditation

Some vocational, technical, or professional schools are not regionally accredited but are accredited by other agencies that are valid and authorized by the US Department of Education. If you are concerned about the accreditation of a school, you can verify the school's standing for yourself by calling the US Department of Education, Accreditation and State Liaison Division, at (202) 708-7417. The general information number for the USDOE is (202) 401-1576.

Illegitimate Accreditation

If an American school does not mention in its catalog that it is accredited by one of the six regional agencies authorized by the USDOE, it might be safe to assume that it is not so accredited. This lack of mention is a warning signal for you to check the school's accreditation. Schools that have accreditation will certainly mention it.

Illegitimate accrediting groups do exist, as do educational programs that exploit their existence. Such groups do not attempt to attain the stamp of approval of the USDOE, but attempt to pass themselves off as being recognized by the federal government. It is unethical for a university to claim accreditation by an unrecognized accrediting agency without revealing that the agency is unrecognized by the USDOE.

Some schools have been known to set up their own accrediting agencies and pretend that the agency is independent. Again, if you are concerned about the accreditation of a school, you should verify the school's standing for yourself. You can do this by calling the US Department of Education, Accreditation and State Liaison Division, at the numbers listed above.

State Approval of Schools and Programs

The United States has both regional and state accrediting agencies. State approval of a college or university is mandatory, not voluntary, and can be a very rigorous process.

It is a mistake to assume that state-approved schools cannot be as effective in helping people reach their career goals as regionally accredited schools. In fact, depending on the circumstances and the quality of the program, state-approved schools can be more effective in a financial sense. The California Council for Private Postsecondary and Vocational Education, for example, has high uniform standards for the California schools it oversees.

State approved schools are known for their moderate cost. They can cost as little as one-third the cost of a regionally accredited degree plan. Many graduates of state-approved programs hold positions in all types of career fields and are highly satisfied with their degrees. You can write to any state's department of education to get a copy of their rules and regulations.

Deciding for Yourself:
State Approved or Regional Accreditation?

The key issue in choosing between a state-approved and a regionally accredited school is to know and understand your own individual needs. If, for instance, you are planning to use your degree in teaching, your degree has to be from a regionally accredited program. You will have to understand and research your own situation in order to make a decision about regional or state accreditation.

There are always a certain number of schools seeking or awaiting various degrees of accreditation. Evaluation processes can be lengthy, and meanwhile, life goes on. Usually, a note in the school catalog or other informative literature indicates that the school considers itself to be offering a quality program that ought to be accredited. Such a note usually indicates good faith; but if you want to be certain, you can check the validity of such a claim by consulting the US Department of Education. For a thorough list of nationally recognized accrediting bodies, see the appendix.

Applying to Schools

6

Herein lies a golden general rule for dealing with admissions counselors, secretaries and advisors: Don't be afraid to ask. If you have questions, they have answers.

IN GENERAL, MOST colleges and universities involved in online higher education have similar requirements for admission. Most online/DL schools emphasize the need for some work experience before you start an online program. Some schools of higher education, especially state-approved schools, will give credit for work experience, mainly if it is within the area of your proposed study.

Schools, colleges, and universities in the United States rely on a battery of standardized entrance examinations to help manage their admissions processes. These exams do not by themselves determine your chances of being accepted by the program, but are part of a formula used by the department, program, or institution to rank candidates. This formula customarily consists of three or more factors in combination:

1. Letters of intent written by you, along with the general state of your admissions materials. American programs will send you many forms to fill out. Make sure you fill out everything, and neatly! Often they will also ask you

for a letter of intent, explaining why you want to be accepted into the program and detailing your professional goals and aspirations.

2. References—letters written in your behalf by other people, recommending you as a good prospect for admissions. Be certain to ask people who know your work well if they will write a positive letter for you. Such letters are usually sent to the school "in confidence," meaning that the writer of the reference is requested by the institution not to show you the letter.

3. Sometimes you will be asked to furnish an example of your work, usually a recent or representative writing sample.

4. Your scores on standardized entrance examinations.

CONTACTING THE ADMISSIONS OFFICE

Whenever you write or speak to a college admissions counselor or a secretary in a department or office, be certain to ask for all the information the institution can give you. Ask specifically for the college catalogue and any other pertinent information, including all application materials and descriptions of and forms for financial aid.

Try to ascertain if admissions decisions are being made at the departmental or institutional level. Many graduate programs in the United States divide the labor: An admissions office attached to the central administrative offices of the school will send out and take delivery of most paperwork, while a committee of actual faculty members in the department will decide who they will accept as students into their department.

It is also a good idea to find out the name or names of the people who will make the decisions affecting your access into the program or department you wish to enter. Sometimes the school's literature will mention the name of the graduate "advisor" or "supervisor." Contact this person to discuss your prospects. Often a secretary will be able to give you this and other information if you ask.

And herein lies a general golden rule for dealing with admissions counselors, secretaries and advisors: Don't be afraid to ask. If you have questions, they have answers. Be polite but persistent, and you will make your name known to the decision-makers before they ever see your letter of application or review your score on an entrance exam.

ENTRANCE EXAMS

The entrance exam has become an American rite of passage: To get into a college, university or graduate school, you usually have to take some form of a standardized test developed and administered by a central body. Most of the exams used by departments and programs in the United States are formulated, administered, and evaluated by Educational Testing Service (ETS), a private company located in Princeton, New Jersey.

There are different kinds of exams and the requirements vary. You will know which exam to take by consulting the information furnished to you by the school you plan to apply to. Find out from the admissions department which test, if any, is required of applicants. Undergraduate admissions procedures usually require you to take either the American College Test (ACT) or Scholastic Achievement Test (SAT). Law schools require the Miller Analogy Test (MAT) or the Law School Admission Test (LSAT). Graduate programs often require the Graduate Management Admission Test (GMAT) or the Graduate Record Examination (GRE)—either the "general skills" test or the "subject area" exam, or both.

Be certain that whatever information you have from ETS or the College Board is the most recent information available. Exam formats and questions are changed continually. Like much else in contemporary life, the best place to go for fast-breaking changes in programs and policies is the World Wide Web. The Web accommodates the fluid nature of the programs and policies of testing agencies like the ACT and SAT. Since so much of what ETS does changes so rapidly, the best place to keep up with the changes is at their Web site, ETS NET: *http://www.ets.org.*

This is a very highly developed and professionally managed site. Here you will find information on all the projects and programs of ETS. You can study the requirements of each exam, try practice questions, and register to take a particular test. There is also a good deal of information on financial aid, including a searchable index called the "College Board's Fund Finder" at *http://www.collegeboard.org/fundfinder/bin/fundfind.1.pl.*

The GRE Exam

The Graduate Record Examination is widely used in American postgraduate education. It is now administered on computer as well as in the old-fashioned "paper-based" manner. It is usually administered at specified locations in the United States three times a year—in October, December, and April.

The *GRE Bulletin* contains information on locations, procedures, and costs. You can obtain a free copy of the Bulletin by writing to ETS at:

GRE
Educational Testing Service
PO Box 6000
Princeton, NJ 08541-6000
E-mail: gre-info@ets.org
Web site: *http://www.gre.org*

The *GRE Bulletin* includes registration forms and other program services information. You may also request from ETS a copy of the General Test Descriptive Booklet, which contains sample questions, a practice test, and test-taking strategies.

The SAT Exam

At present, the SAT exam has three parts: verbal, mathematics, and a "plus" section (a combination of verbal and math tests). The SAT exams are administered by a subdivision of ETS called The College Board. To find out more about the SAT exams, you can write to the following address:

College Board SAT Program
PO Box 6200
Princeton, NJ 08541-6200
Web site: *http://www.collegeboard.org*

Ask them to send you the *SAT Program Registration Bulletin*. This bulletin, which can often be found in the counseling or admissions offices of your local college, is free to students who plan to take the SAT exam. On their Web site, you will find an online version of the *Registration Bulletin*, which has an "International Edition."

The ACT Exam

The ACT test has four sections: English, mathematics, reading, and science reasoning. The ACT (American College Testing) program is also administered by ETS. Like the SAT, it is written in English only and is administered only at certain times of the year at designated locations. Contact the ACT offices at:

ACT—Educational Testing Service
Princeton, NJ 08541
Web site: *http://www.ets.org*

PLANNING AHEAD

There are fees to pay when you register for these exams. It is a good idea to plan far ahead for entrance exams. You should begin finding and filling out applications one year in advance of

Photo by McBee

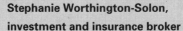

**Stephanie Worthington-Solon,
investment and insurance broker**

I thought I could do anything I want, but I found out
that working full time and going to college full time
just does not work. The idea of getting my MBA
crossed my mind many times, but after the hard work
I had to put forward to complete my bachelor's degree
while working, I realized that it is a dream which might
never come true. Online higher education and the flex-
ibility it offers has changed my mind. I sincerely believe that my dream of getting an MBA is not far away.

the time you want to enter a program. In the United States this
usually means that you get busy in September or October for an
autumn entrance in the next academic year. Online schools tend
to be more flexible than tradtional schools when it comes to application deadlines, but it is best to prepare well in advance.

ETS provides sample tests for its exams, but there aren't
really any official guidelines for studying to take them. This kind
of exam tests depth knowledge, so you cannot really cram for an
entrance exam in a short period of time. You should be wary of
guides that guarantee higher results. There do exist small companies that purport to help you, for a fee, to prepare. One such

company, Prepmaster Review, Inc., holds seminars and packages self-study materials. You can reach them at:

Prepmaster Review
University Station
PO Box 7555
Austin, TX 78713-9821
Web site: *http://www.prepmaster.com*

You can retake any exam administered by ETS. The latest exam taken will "bankrupt" (that is, replace) previous test results. About the best advice you will ever hear for taking an entrance exam is this piece of simple common sense: Get a decent night's sleep the night before you take the exam and eat breakfast in the morning. Nervousness and anxiety are your worst enemies.

DEGREES

Determine what sort of degree you are interested in before you seek admission. Undergraduate degrees include the associate degree and the bachelor's degree. Postgraduate degrees include the master's degree and doctoral degrees.

Associate Degree

The main requirement for entrance into an associate degree program is a high school diploma or GED (general equivalency diploma) or GCE (general certificate of education). If you need information about a GED program, contact the GED Office in your state, or write:

American Council on Education
GED Testing Service
One Dupont Circle, Suite 250
Washington, DC 20036-1163

Bachelor's Degree

The general requirements for a bachelor's degree are:

- high school diploma, GED, or GCE

- official transcript from your high school

- letters of recommendation

- work experience: most online/DL schools require work experience in addition to a high school diploma

Master's Degree

The requirements for admission for a master's degree are more demanding:

- work experience: most online/DL schools require that the applicant have work experience ranging between two to five years

- bachelor's degree in the same area of study or related area

- grade point average (GPA) of 2.00 or above on a scale of 4.00

- official transcript from your undergraduate school

- letters of recommendation from your instructors or people who have worked with you closely

- GMAT or GRE: Business schools usually require that you take the GMAT; engineering schools require the GRE. If the school requires a score of 1100 for admission to the MBA program, you can calculate your score by using the following formula:

$$\text{Score} = (\text{GPA} \times 2) + \text{GMAT score}$$

For instance, if your GPA is 3.00, you have to score 500 in the GMAT test to meet the school requirement of 1100 points:

$$1100 = (300 \times 2) + \text{GMAT score}$$

Doctoral Studies

A doctorate is the highest degree that can be earned. Schools vary in their requirements, but most require the following:

- work experience of at least five years

- master's degree

- grade point average of at least 3.00 on a scale of 4.00

- official transcripts from previous academic institutions attended

- three letters of recommendation

APPLICATION PROCEDURES

The procedure starts with filling out an application form. You can download it from the college's Web site, if one is available, or request one by e-mail. Include the proper documents and processing fees, then mail the packet to the admissions office.

Processing fees for admission vary, starting from about $25.

Transcripts

You will need to present official copies of transcripts from any colleges or universities you have attended. Usually, you must contact the school from which you graduated. Transcripts are sent directly from one school to the other to protect the integrity of the process.

Letters of Recommendation

You will usually be asked to provide three letters of recommendation from your teachers or people who have worked closely with you. These are usually written and sent "in confidence" to the school by the person providing the reference.

Interview

The interview is another tradition that education doesn't quite know what to do with in the new, online world of distance learning. Some schools require that you visit the campus for an interview. If you live far from the school, you might be able to negotiate around this requirement, or substitute for it with a phone interview.

Like the job search in the business world, the application process in the academic world can be a bit onerous. Some schools do not automatically grant admission, and some schools admit only a certain percentage of applicants. It is a good idea to prepare applications in twos or threes: two packets to schools that are a "stretch" for you (a school with very high standards, well known, probably expensive); two or three to schools that will probably accept you and that you would like to attend; and two or three "fallback" schools (easy for you to get into and attend, and that you will be happy attending if your first choices do not accept you). Again, many online schools are faster than traditional schools in the admission process.

Credit for Life Experience

Some schools might give you some credit for related work experience. It does not hurt to ask. That could save you some time and money.

Credit by Examinations

If you feel there is a subject in your program that you know very well, you can ask to be tested. If you pass, you don't have to take the course. There is usually a charge for that, but it is still far less than the cost of taking the course.

Financing
Your Online Degree

7

Students should view an education like a financial investment that will yield a return for a lifetime. Be creative, courageous, and persistent in pursuing financing options for your degree.

T HE PRICE OF education in the United States is rapidly rising. Tuition fees especially are becoming a significant impediment to all forms of higher education, but housing, books, food, and everything else is on the rise as well. Not everyone has the funds to cover these expenses, but fortunately, it is still possible to subsidize the cost of higher education. There are three broad categories of financial aid: grants and scholarships, educational loans, and work study.

GRANTS AND SCHOLARSHIPS

Scholarships are moneys given to students to cover all or part of their educational expenses. A scholarship is more or less a gift of money—it does not have to be paid back. Almost all colleges and universities maintain some form or other of scholarship funding. Competition for scholarships is intense, and growing ever more so. Although all schools have varying definitions of what it means to be a deserving or entitled student, scholarships and grants are usually based on academic achievements or financial need, or both.

Another form of financial grant is the *research fund.* Research moneys are often supplied by individuals, businesses or organizations interested in particular research projects. This type of support is typically found in larger universities staffed by faculties specifically devoted to research, or in regular universities with large numbers of graduate students. Often a noted faculty member receives a grant, which he or she then uses to set up and manage an experimental facility or project. Graduate students working for such projects benefit in a trickle-down fashion by receiving cash stipends, tuition remission, or other forms of payment for their participation.

To qualify for a scholarship or grant, you must of course apply for it. Colleges and universities publish lists of available grants and scholarships, including detailed explanations of eligibility and requirements. Increasingly, these documents are maintained on Web sites managed by the college's financial aid department at the college's homepage.

You can find a comprehensive list of American colleges and universities at *http://www.clas.ufl.edu/CLAS/american-universities.html.* (Note: This address is case sensitive.) This Web site is perhaps the best place to go for the most recent information on a particular college or university's programs and policies, including the state of its financial aid resources and practices.

The various publications of the *Peterson's Guide* series are probably the most authoritative guides to colleges and universities in the United States. Guides published by Peterson's are still regarded as authoritative and up-to-date, though the competition is on the rise from online companies that offer the same services. You would be wise, however, to complement any other guides you may consult by going to the specific web page of the individual college you are interested in. You can do that by pointing your web browser at the Web site noted.

It may also be prudent to run a topical search on one of the major search engines, such as Yahoo! or Lycos or Webcrawler, for information on financial aid and grants. Do this by entering "financial aid" or "scholarships" or similar keywords in the subject slot or term prompt on the search page. The more specific you can be with your keyword(s), the more manageable will be the results. As search engines become ever more sophisticated, the number of "hits" they generate for any given term can quickly—indeed, instantaneously—grow to overwhelming proportions. It's a good rule to "narrow" your search in every way possible.

The fastWEB (Financial Aid Search Through the WEB) is a particularly excellent search index on the World Wide Web for financial aid sources (find it at *http://www.studentservices.com/fastweb*). This scholarship search includes over 180,000 private sector scholarships, fellowships, grants, and loans in its database. The fastWEB is now available to you free through the World Wide Web. To use fastWEB, complete the online profile forms. After the forms are complete, fastWEB responds within fifteen minutes with a list of matching award programs.

The Grants Register

The Grants Register is a good reference book to get to know. A venerated compendium of sources of financial aid, it is usually found in the reference section of a good library. It is published fairly frequently. Always ask for the most recent edition. *The Grants Register* lists grants, scholarships, and like awards available to individuals pursuing a degree (baccalaureate, masters, doctorate, and so on). Award-giving bodies vary from small trusts and organizations to larger corporations and educational institutions. The *Register* is arranged by country and subject; you can look under the country you are currently in or would like to study in, and also under their particular subject area.

The awards can be highly idiosyncratic. It would not be unusual, for example, to find an entry that requires the applicant to

> **Rachel Gregory, working mother**
> I am a twenty-year-old single mother with two young kids. I have to work full time to support them and going to a traditional school is almost impossible for me. Therefore I find this new way of learning and pursuing my career is the only path available to me. I am interested in a health care career, and I am currently contacting various schools listed in this book to choose the best program for me.
>
> I never thought I would be able to go to school, work full time, and still find time to spend with my kids. I think this is a great opportunity for me and for the majority of single mothers out there.

be the second son of a war veteran who intends to do field research on as-yet-unclassified bugs in the rain forests of Brazil. Applications can also vary, from a mere letter describing a program of study to seemingly endless standardized forms. Still, there is a *lot* of money to be given away by these organizations, and it is well worth a couple of hours of careful study in the library.

The Admission Office

Whenever you write or speak to a college admissions counselor or a secretary in a department or office, be certain to ask for all the information the institution can give you. Mainly, ask for the financial aid application in order to find out how much money you qualify for.

Other Sources of Financial Aid

Some companies, like Microsoft, AT&T, and others, offer academic grants. AT&T has recently announced $1 million in grants for global distance learning programs. Microsoft offers millions of dollars to schools developing IT programs. Once again, the best avenue to recent information is one of the web search engines mentioned earlier.

One of the very best sites on the World Wide Web from which to start a search for financial aid sources is FinAid, The Financial Aid Page, maintained by Mark Kantrowitz, at *http://www.finaid.org*. Kantrowitz, author of *The Prentice Hall Guide to Scholarships for Math and Science Students*, has gathered together on one page an eminently readable, continuously updated set of reference points for financial aid. This is a very intelligent overall view of what's available on the web. It is highly recommended as a point of origin in a search for the right grant or fellowship.

STUDENT LOANS

The United States has an extensive student loan program, administered at both the federal and state levels. Student who fulfill the requirements are entitled to educational loans that are comparatively generous in their interest rates and repayment schemes.

Basically, the process of getting a loan depends upon federal guarantees of private loans. The federal government underwrites regular student loans at commercial banks. It also pays the interest while you are in school. Repayment on a student loan starts six months after you graduate, as do the interest charges. Early into the repayment schedule, exemptions are customarily granted for financial hardship. If you cannot begin repayments because you don't have a job, for example, you may be able to delay the startup of the repayment by applying for a deferment.

There are no permanent deferments, however. Lenient payment schedules are sometimes offered to people who select certain professional situations after graduation, such as teaching in designated low-income areas, Peace Corps work, military service, or enrollment in further job training. But the borrowed money is still due, of course, and you cannot escape repayment of a student loan with interest even if you file for bankruptcy. If you fail to pay back the loan, the government could deduct your monthly payment from your tax returns.

The repayment period is usually up to ten years, but you can consolidate your loans and extend the repayment period for up to thirty years. If your income does not allow you to make the monthly payment, you have an option to use the Income Sensitive Repayment Plan. Intended to encourage adult students to go back to school, the plan allows you to pay as little as 4 percent of your monthly income and to extend the repayment period to thirty years. If the loan is not paid after thirty years, it is canceled and you are not obligated to pay it back. In case of death, the student's family does not inherit the loan and does not have to pay it back.

Another repayment option is now available to students. You can repay part of the loan by doing some community work in connection with the Americorps program. The financial aid office in any nearby college or university will have full details on Americorps and other programs, available for the asking.

The federal government has recently passed new regulations that simplify the process of borrowing money for higher education. The various definitions of "needy student" have been somewhat relaxed to make it easier for more people to qualify for educational loans.

Federal Student Loans

At present there are two main types of student loans: the Federal Subsidized Stafford Loan and the Federal Unsubsidized Stafford Loan.

The Federal Subsidized Stafford Loan This loan is available, in whole or part, to students who demonstrate financial need.

Loan Limits: $8,500 per nine-month loan period.

Aggregate Limit: $65,000.

Interest Rates: The government pays interest while student is in school.

Variable: (T-Bill + 3.1%)

Fixed Rate: 7%, 8%, or 9% (for borrowers prior to 7/1/88)

Processing Fees: Up to 4%

Note: Interest rates will vary. Consult with your school's financial aid office to ascertain which loan program is for you.

The Federal Unsubsidized Stafford Loan This loan is available to students, in whole or part, who do not meet the need requirements for the Federal Subsidized Stafford Loan, or to students who wish to borrow in addition to their Federal Subsidized Stafford Loan eligibility.

Loan Limits: $8,500 minus Subsidized Stafford Loan eligibility, per nine-month loan period.

Aggregate Limit: $138,500 including amounts borrowed from Subsidized Stafford Loan.

Interest Rates: Interest accrues. The student is responsible for payment or deferment of interest while in school.

Variable Rate: (T-Bill + 3.1%), Capped at 8.25% for new borrowers after 7/1/94.

Fixed Rate: 7%, 8%, or 9% (for borrowers prior to 7/1/88)

Processing Fees: Up to 4%

Note: Interest rates will vary. Consult with your school's financial aid office to ascertain which loan program is for you.

For full details on the process of applying for loans, contact the financial aid office of the school you plan to attend. See also *Peterson's*, ETS, or the Kantrowitz Web pages.

Qualifying for Loans

Student loans are intended for students to cover the cost of their education, and should only be used for that purpose. The general guidelines to qualify for financial aid are as follows:

Accredited School The student should be enrolled in an accredited school recognized by one of the accrediting agencies recognized by the US Department of Education. (Note: To qualify for a federal loan you must attend a school that has been accredited by one of the agencies recognized by the USDOE. If you attend a school that has been accredited exclusively by a state, you will not qualify for a loan underwritten by the federal government.)

Full-Time or Half-Time A student has to be enrolled in school full-time or at least half-time. Undergraduate students must be enrolled in at least 12 credit hours per semester to be considered full-time, or at least 6 credit hours a semester to be considered half-time. Graduate students must be enrolled in 9 credit hours to be considered full-time, and 5 to 6 credit hours to be considered half-time. The money available for full-time study is more than the money available for half-time study, and graduate students can expect to receive more money than undergraduate students.

Good Academic Standing A student has to maintain good academic standing. For an undergraduate student, that means a grade point average (GPA) of at least 2.00 on a scale of 4.00. Graduate students pursuing their master's or doctorate degrees should maintain a GPA of at least 3.00 on a scale of 4.00 points.

Loan Default To qualify for a loan, a student must not be in default for another educational loan. You may now apply for financial aid by completing and submitting the Free Application for Federal Student Aid (FAFSA) over the Internet, by visiting the US Department of Education Web site at *http://www.fafsa.ed.gov.*

WORK STUDY

Work study is another form of financial aid to consider. Work study programs are set up so that qualified students can work in college in return for a wage or for tuition waivers. Contact a financial aid counselor at your school for more information.

ADDITIONAL FINANCIAL SOURCES

Assistantships

Many colleges and universities offer assistantships for graduate students. I am not aware of any online school offering work study programs or assistantships to its online students. If you have computer skills or some experience teaching, however, ask if such a program is available.

Employer Funding

More and more organizations are offering new kinds of help to their employees, so your employer should be the first party you turn to in search of financial assistance to help cover the cost of your higher education. Check your employer's policy on continuing education. Many organizations will reimburse your costs if you pass the course with a grade of B or better, especially if your course of study pertains directly to your job.

Employers are coming to recognize that they have a responsibility to train tomorrow's workers in an information economy. Current and future jobs are knowledge based. Only companies that understand this will be able to excel in the future. A company that does not support its employees in education definitely does not have a long-term vision and might not exist in business when you graduate.

Miscellaneous Sources

Like so much else nowadays, becoming a student is an entrepreneurial project. In today's world, everyone is a self-financier. Try to be creative, courageous, and persistent. Learn to write a letter that impresses the people who hold the purse strings.

Many students have received substantial help from employers, unions, local philanthropists, pastors, the phone company, relatives, student senates, national societies, deans, and department chairpersons. If you can think of someone to ask, go ahead and ask. You might be surprised at how willing some people and institutions can be to help you pursue your dreams.

8

Online Educational Resources

The Internet can provide you with educational resources far beyond your local library, large or small. It is like having the world's libraries at your fingertips.

 VEN BEFORE YOU start going to school on the Internet, you can investigate the wide range of educational resources available. You'll find libraries filled with information, and you may even find free classes.

THE VIRTUAL LIBRARY

Libraries are essential tools for any student participating in an online program. On the Internet, students enjoy resources beyond the limitation of a local university's library.

ERIC

Web site: *http://ericir.syr.edu*

One of the most important sites for educators on the Internet is the Educational Resources Information Center (ERIC), the world's largest source of educational information. ERIC's *Indexes for Research in Education,* and *Current Index to Journals in*

Education, have been standards in libraries for over thirty years. ERIC is federally funded by the US Department of Education, which also supports the ERIC clearinghouses. These provide varying levels of service to people in the field of education. The AskERIC virtual library has lesson plans, ERIC Digests (short essays by professionals on "hot topics"), ERIC publications, reference tools, Internet guides and directories, government information, and archives for education-related discussion lists on Usenet. ERIC is of special interest to educators and media specialists, but it's also a great resource for parents.

CARL

Web site: *http://www.carl.org*

CARL, which began life as the Colorado Alliance of Research Libraries, is now CARL Corporation, a giant library management system. More than 625 libraries are currently on the CARL system. The CARL UnCover document delivery service offers access to over 4 million articles. At CARL, Journal Graphics will mail or fax television news transcripts from their archives. You must have a credit card or deposit account with CARL to receive information.

GoMlink

Web site: *http://www.umd.umich.edu/lib/um-dlp.html*

GoMlink is an electronic public library maintained by the University of Michigan Library. It is arranged by broad subject categories: business and economics; computers and technology; education; entertainment and recreation; environment; government and politics; health and nutrition; humanities; libraries and librarianship; Michigan; news services, newsletters and journals; a reference desk; science; social issues and social services; and the Internet and its other resources. This service is one of the better reference desks on the Internet and one of the best starting points for new Internet users; experienced users can browse its vast subject collections. A public client is available.

Library of Congress

Web site: *http://www.loc.gov*

This site contains an enormous amount of information not only about the Library of Congress itself but also about the US government and American culture and history. There are links to Library of Congress publications, the Center for Books, Library Services for the Blind and Physically Handicapped, and many more. Other features include:

- Research tools: Resources for researchers and information professionals. These include the catalogs of the Library of Congress and other libraries, databases on special topics, and other Library of Congress Internet resources.

- Library services: Resources for libraries, information professionals, and researchers. These include Acquisitions, Cataloging, Preservation, Research, Special Programs, Standards, and access to the catalogs of the Library of Congress and other libraries.

- Full-text access to current bills under consideration in the US House of Representatives and Senate.

ONLINE/DL EDUCATION WEB SITES

Following is a short listing of Web sites that present basic information about distance and online education. To find more sites, do a search with the keywords "online education," "distance learning," or "distance education."

United States Distance Learning Association

Web site: *http://www.usdla.org*

This is a nonprofit association formed to promote the development and application of distance learning for education and training. The constitutents it serves include K through 12 education, higher education, continuing education, corporate training, and military and government training.

USDLA convened a National Policy Forum in July 1991 to develop and publish a set of National Policy Recommendations that have been the basis of legislative and administrative proposals in education and telecommunications policy.

The association has become the leading source of information and recommendations for government agencies, congress, industry, and those developing distance learning programs. In 1993, USDLA began establishing chapters in all fifty states. In addition, USDLA holds annual meetings with leaders of distance learning programs in Europe and Asia.

University of Houston Clear Lake

Web site: *http://129.7.160.115/COURSE/DISTEDFAQ/Disted_FAQ.html*

This site provides good answers to Frequently Asked Questions (FAQs) about distance education. It also provides information on distance education oganizations, issues in distance education, Web-based training, conferences, online journals about distance education, distance education general links, directories, clearinghouses, libraries, and online courseware.

University of Wisconsin-Extension
Distance Education Clearinghouse

Web site: *http://www.uwex.edu/disted/home.html*

This site has a wealth of information and links, including such topics as current news in distance education; articles, bibliographies, and resources; conferences; funding and legislation; a distance education systemwide interactive electronic newsletter; information on technologies such as interactive delivery systems, networks, compressed video, and satellite; distance education definitions, glossaries, and introductory materials; and links to products, associations, and more distance education sites.

Academe This Week

Web site: *http://www.chronicle.merit.edu*

Academe This Week is an online service of the *Chronicle of Higher Education*. It includes the most comprehensive and up-to-date listing of academic jobs in North America. If you are looking for work in a university or college, or you want to know what such job descriptions look like, this is where to go. You'll find job postings, a table of contents for the current hard-copy issue of the *Chronicle*, events in academia, portions of the statistical almanac, bestselling books on college campuses, and more from this standard resource.

FREE ONLINE COURSES

It is hard to believe that you can get anything free these days, but it's possible on the Internet. Some colleges offer a free trial course for a week or two. Try one to get an idea of what you can expect from online/DL classes.

There's no telling what will be available on the Net tomorrow or next month or next year. Search the Web using the keywords "free" or "free+course" or "free+college" and see what comes up. The result might surprise you.

One virtual university offers free online education right now. The nonprofit, tax-exempt school, Spectrum Universal, is sponsored largely by CompuServe, and the instructors are volunteers.

Lynn Hirst, high school teacher

I was interested in getting my master's degree in occupational therapy, but this study area was not available in my hometown college. The closest college that offers such a course of study is 120 miles away. I thought of moving, but I couldn't afford to quit my job and take chances in looking for a new job. So I put my goal on hold.

Then I came across this book at the local bookstore. It gave me all the information I needed to pursue a degree over the Internet—universities, Web sites, e-mail addresses, degrees, cost, contacts, and so on. I would highly recommend this book to anyone who would like to pursue a degree in the comfort of their own home. What a lifesaver!

Following is a brief description of the school's mission as stated on their homepage:

Spectrum Universal is a non-profit 501 (c)(3) tax-exempt organization with a long history of involvement in community service projects and education.

In the 1960's, our founders were active supporters of
the early Free Clinic movement. They established counseling centers in California and New York, a suicide prevention
hotline, a "safe house" for juvenile runaways, and a drug
education workshop years before it became politically fash-
ionable to "Just Say No." They were among the earliest ad-
vocates of the modern home schooling movement.

In the 1970's, we founded the Discovery Center, which
provided free and low-cost classes and workshops to thousands. We pioneered one of the first "interactive" learning
programs, using an ordinary touchtone telephone and answering machine, years before computers began to appear
on desktops.

With the advent of the first affordable computers and
modems, we continued to explore low-cost ways to offer
classes and workshops via electronic bulletin boards. In
1988, we began development of "Digital Professor," the first
known application that used Computer Telephony for educational purposes. In 1992, this program was a finalist in
Educom's Software Innovation Awards. Later that year, it
was recognized in the Software Star Search compiled by
Computer Reseller News, a leading trade publication.

In the Fall of 1995, we introduced "Web Class," a
WWW-based application that simulates a virtual reality
classroom complete with a Homework Calendar, Class Discussion forum, Gradebook, and "virtual desks" for each student. This exciting new approach to learning has received
favorable mention in more than 200 online publications, as
well as conventional, and newspapers including *Information
Week*, *Seattle Times*, *London Guardian*, *St. Petersburg Press*
(Moscow), *Folha de Sao Paulo* (Brazil), and *Zambia Post*
(Africa).

Today, we remain dedicated to the goal of making
knowledge freely available to our students throughout the

global village and we are continuing to explore new ways to promote world peace, prosperity, and enlightenment through community service and far-sighted programs that can make the world a better place.

To learn more, visit the school at their Web site: *http://www.vu.org*.

Special Considerations
for International Students

9

An international professional basically has to give up his or her life to
go to the United States to pursue a higher degree.

ITH A GLOBAL link, instructors and students will someday participate in educational programs and projects in any country, from any country. Such diversity and interaction will enrich the educational process and give it a new dimension. Internet education is a golden opportunity for the citizens of the world. Unfortunately, citizens of some countries cannot enjoy such a technology because of technical difficulties or for financial or political reasons.

North American accredited college degrees have a good reputation all over the world. But, like everything else, the cost is rising. Obtaining a four-year college degree in the United States can cost between $30,000 and $50,000 dollars, plus another $30,000 to $40,000 dollars minimum as living expenses for a four-year period. Add to these figures the forgone wages and benefits of an interrupted career, and you see that an international professional has basically to give up his or her life to go to the United States to pursue a higher degree.

Such a move involves many costs and sacrifices—the cost of traveling, of living in the United States, of owning a car and

Amal Ghazi, beauty shop owner, Amman, Jordan

I never had the chance to go to college after my graduation from high school because I had to start working to help support my large family. I am now running a beauty shop, but I need to know more about business. I know I need more education and training, but I cannot afford to leave the shop or close its doors while I am at school.

I have a computer in the shop to run my business. I am utilizing it now to take accounting and business courses in the United States over the Internet, right here in my shop. I never thought that could be done. I am very pleased with this opportunity.

insurance, the sacrifice of being away from family and loved ones, and so on. It is not uncommon for an international student to spend hundreds of dollars on telephone calls each month to talk to family and loved ones back home.

Another difficulty is learning the language and culture of North American life, especially the slang. Most international students have a good command of the English language, but when it comes to accent and dialect, some students will struggle to communicate with their colleges and instructors. Many international professionals make sacrifices to learn about and adapt to new cultural expectations. It is not an easy task. Online education provides an option to international professionals that allows them to avoid a myriad of expensive frustrations.

SELECTING A SCHOOL

International students must learn how schools operate in the United States. This may be very different from the way schools operate in their own countries. Americans who choose to study abroad will also have to figure out how schools operate in other countries and will want to make sure that credit earned abroad is recognized in the United States.

Accreditation

The accreditation system in the United States is unique. Although many different colleges and universities with state accreditation have quality programs, international students should seek admission to schools that are accredited by agencies approved by the US Department of Education. A list of those agencies can be found in chapter 5. International students should also verify the accreditation status with the Ministry of Education in their own countries. Then, take these steps:

- Contact the schools you are considering— communicating via e-mail is easiest.

- Ask for catalogs to be mailed to you.

- Contact the US accreditation agency and verify the school's accreditation status. Cross-check the school's accreditation status with the ministry of education in your country and ask how they rate the schools you have selected.

Troy Yu, assistant manager, import and export company, China

I graduated from Nanjing University and am now holding a job as an assistant manager in an import and export company. I always felt that having an MBA from the United States would help me get promoted in my job. When I turned to the Internet for help, I was overwhelmed by the hundreds of universities and thousands of courses I found. Then I ordered this book. and was pleased to find so much information in one place—it's a real time saver. With the information in this book I can turn my dream into reality.

Financial Aid

Financial aid is not available for international students. You must be an American citizen or a permanent resident of the United States to qualify for financial aid.

Scholarships or grants for international students are extremely limited, so make a thorough search. Check with organizations and institutions in your own country for scholarships or financial aid.

Internet Access

Make sure the college or university you select uses the Internet for accessing the degree program you are interested in, rather than having their own proprietary internal computer system or network. An internal computer network will cost more to access; your phone calls to access the school's network will be considered international, which will add considerably to your expenses.

If you live in a country where Internet access is not easily available to individuals' homes, try to use the facilities of a large corporation or an organization that has Internet access.

Ask the college to respond to your messages by e-mail, fax, or telephone, as regular airmail to various countries takes too long.

Proctoring

If you are living outside the United States, finding an entity or an individual to proctor your exams might be a problem; the college might have a hard time approving such a proctor. To avoid such a potential problem, check with the American Embassy or any American institution in your country to find a person there who can proctor your exam. The college will prefer such a setup.

Videotapes

If the college you will attend uses videotapes as one of its delivery media, you will encounter an extra obstacle: The United States uses the NTSC system, while most of the world uses PAL or SECAM systems. You will need a facility to convert the tapes from NTSC to PAL or SECAM. This can be expensive. Try asking the college to do that for you before they send the tape; most large colleges have an instructional media center that is equipped to do such a conversion.

10

Finding a Job Online

The spectrum of education and work on the Internet is as wide as the world and yet as close as your personal computer.

O NCE YOU'VE FINISHED your dream degree online, your next step will probably be to look for a job where you can put your new knowledge to use. The Internet offers a wealth of job hunting resources, from tips on how to write a resume to lists of current job openings all around the world.

GETTING STARTED

A good first step in any job hunt is to evaluate yourself: your education, qualifications, goals, expertise, drive, and resources. Ask yourself the following questions:

1. What am I qualified to do?

2. What do I like to do?

3. What do others need done?

4. Will I be self-employed or employed by another?

5. Am I willing to relocate?

The answers to these questions will help you to define your ideal job.

Writing Your Resumé

Once you have determined what it is you want to do, you will need to write a resumé of your qualifications and goals. This document should be impressive. Rather than selling a product or a service, this time you will be selling yourself. Don't sell yourself short; reflect quality, honesty, knowledge, and professionalism in your resumé.

You can write your resumé yourself or hire somebody with experience to prepare it for you. You can find valuable assistance online. Lycos, for example, offers a complete site called "Resumé Writing." If you don't already have a resumé or vita prepared, this is an excellent place to start. You can also do an online search using the keyword "resume."

References

References are an excellent way of selling yourself to a prospective employer. Ask people who know you and your work abilities well if they would be willing to serve as a reference should a prospective employer want to speak to them about your qualifications. Sometimes employers may ask for letters of recommendation. In this case, ask your references to keep your letter of recommendation on file in case you need them to send a letter to more than one employer. It is best if your references have known you for more than two years. A reference for employment and skills should be current—within the last five years.

Create a Homepage

Selling yourself has never been easier than it is on the Internet. Build your own homepage and advertise *you*. If you plan to be

Networking or Not Working

The principle "Networking or Not Working" applies on the Net just as it does in other types of employment. You want the world to know that you have the qualifications, the education, and the knowledge it takes to get the job done. Here are some tips for getting your name out there.

- Reward and congratulate yourself by announcing in your community newspaper that you have graduated. Send your picture and a short article about yourself and your degree to the local newspapers. Most local newspapers will print such an announcement free of charge.
- Write an article about your experience in online education and see if your local newspaper will print it.
- Tell all your friends and the people you know about your new academic accomplishment. They will spread the word for you.
- Read newspaper employment ads and attend job fairs.
- Subscribe to one or more online discussion groups related to your subject of expertise. Group members discuss recent issues in the field and sometimes post job openings that they know about. In the unlikely event that you cannot find a discussion group pertaining to your field, create your own group and ask others to join you.

self-employed, a homepage is an excellent way to attract potential clients. It's also a good way for employers or headhunters to find you.

List your qualifications, goals, and resources. You may even want to put your picture on your page (make sure you smile!). It is important to design a page that best uses your skills and creative abilities. A well-laid-out, creative, and technically engineered homepage is a good illustration of your computer and organizational skills.

You can hire a professional to build your page for you. A simple page may run $200 to $300. I think this investment is worth it. If you like to do things yourself, there is a site that will help you build your own homepage, step by step, without programming knowledge: *http://www.tripod.com.*

Promote Your Homepage

Once you have created your homepage, you will need to post it on the Net. The Internet is full of advertisers; everyone is after the navigator's attention. People who surf the Internet are impatient— there is so much to see, and you have only seconds to capture their attention. It is not good enough to have a well-designed homepage. It also has to be listed with many search engines, so people can find you.

There are many places to promote your site; some are free, others charge a small fee. Almost every search engine allows you to add your site free. One of the most popular search engines is Yahoo!, which can generate many inquiries for you.

Another way to advertise your site efficiently is to send it to a promoter, who will list it with most search engines for a small fee. This will save you a lot of time. For more information, visit *http://www.broadcaster.co.uk/index.htm.*

The most used search engines are:

http://www.webcrawler.com
http://www.yahoo.com
http://www.altavista.digital.com
http://www.excite.com
http://www.hotbot.com
http://www.lycos.com
http://www.infoseek.com

**Scott Wells,
computer programmer**

I am studying computer programming and soon [will earn] my associate degree in computer programming and network management. I have been offered a job as a computer programmer with a national company in the health care field. My company pays all the fees for furthering my education. I am pleased to be able to further my education in the computer field without missing time from work. I am learning a lot at school while enhancing my experience at work. This is like having the best of both worlds. I can't imagine doing this without online education.

http://www.looksmart.com
http://www.trafficboost.com
http://www.broadcaster.co.uk/fullorder.htm

HOW TO DO AN ONLINE JOB SEARCH

Job hunting on the Internet is time consuming, but it's more efficient and simple than traditional job hunting methods.

Each of the search engines has a section for employment, and you can search for the specific job or career you are interested in. Be sure to use the appropriate keywords. For example, type in "computer programming" to generate a list of opportunities in that field. If you want a broader search, type in the word "career" or "employment" or even "jobs". You can then narrow down the search if you type + in the field next to it. For example, if you are hunting for a job in the educational field, you would type in your search: "careers+education". This should find leads to jobs in many educational fields.

Online Career Center (OCC)

Web site: *http://www.occ.com/occ*

This an excellent place to begin your search for an online career.

AOL Netfind

Web site: *http://www.aol.com/netfind/timesavers/job.html*

This is another excellent place to search for jobs. It can also help you figure out which jobs are right for you, put together a winning resumé, learn how to interview, and learn how and where to look for jobs.

Lycos

Web site: *http://www.lycos.com*

Using the search engine Lycos and the keyword "careers" opens a whole world of possibilities. You can search for careers using the specific title of the job you are interested in, or go through the list they have compiled. This site includes related topics to search such as: Career Web Guide; Community Guide: Special Fairs for the Unemployed; and Personal Homepages: Careers Online. It also contains various other topics too numerous to mention here. Check it out.

Excite

Web site: *http://www.excite.com*

Excite is yet another good employment resource. Sponsored by OCC and the Monster Board, this site offers "fast, free, and easy access to more than 100,000 current job opportunities." It also offers information on education, resumés, job searches, and careers.

A FINAL WORD

This is only a small sample of the job hunting opportunities and resources available on the Net. There are many other sites and search engines, which are not less important, available to you. The spectrum of education and work on the Internet is as wide as the world and yet as close as your personal computer. And things will even get better with time.

I would like to conclude this book with the following quote from the Council on Competitiveness:

> The information infrastructure of the twenty-first century will enable all Americans to access information and communicate with each other easily, reliably, securely, and cost-effectively in any medium, voice, data, image, or video, any time, anywhere. This capability will enhance the productivity of work and lead to dramatic improvements in social services, education, and entertainment.

Part Two

Listing of Schools

HOW TO READ
THE SCHOOL INFORMATION

I have organized the information about schools that offer online/
distance learning (online/DL) so that it is easy to find what you
are looking for. Each listing is formatted as follows:

School: Name of the college or university.

ID: This number is assigned for easy reference.

Type: Schools are either public or private. A *public* school is
usually funded by the state; a *private* school is owned by
a person or group of people and receives no government
funding.

Established: The year the college was established.

Accreditation: The school's accreditation status.
- Regional: The highest accreditation status for a college
  or university; optional in the United States.
- Other Valid Accreditation: Some schools are accredited by
  another agency, such as the Distance Education Training
  Council (DETC). There are many other valid accreditation
  agencies authorized by the US Department of Education.
- State Approved: A school that has the approval of the
  state to operate (mandatory)

Financial Aid: Some schools offer federal financial aid for
online/DL education (a regional accredited college is required to offer financial aid for on-campus students).

Total Students: Total school enrollment.

Online/DL Students: Number of students enrolled in the
distance learning program.

Undergrad Cr. Hr. Cost: Cost per semester credit hour for
undergraduate students.

Grad Cr. Hr. Cost: Cost per semester credit hour for graduate students.

Web Site: The URL for the school.

E-mail: The school's e-mail address.

Toll-Free: The 800 or 888 number for information about the school, if available. These numbers are not available in all states, and are not available overseas.

Phone: The school's phone number.

Fax: The school's fax number.

Address: The distance learning department address, if available; otherwise, the school address.

General Courses: Indicates whether the school offers general courses online/DL.

Certificates: Indicates whether or not the school offers a certificate program online/DL.

Associate: Indicates whether or not the school offers an associate degree program.

- **Associate Hours:** Number of semester credit hours needed to fulfill associate degree. See note, page 97.
- **Associate Cost:** Total cost of associate degree. See note, page 97.

Bachelor's: Indicates whether or not the school offers a bachelor's degree program.

- **Bachelor's Hours:** Number of semester credit hours needed to fulfill bachelor's degree. See note, page 97.
- **Bachelor's Cost:** Total cost of bachelor's degree. See note, page 97.

Master's: Indicates whether or not the school offers a master's degree program.

- **Master's Hours:** Number of semester credit hours needed to fulfill master's degree. See note, page 97.
- **Master's Cost:** Total cost of master's degree. See note, page 97.

PhD: Indicates whether or not the school offers a doctoral program.

- **PhD Hours:** Number of semester credit hours needed to fulfill doctoral degree. See note, page 97.
- **PhD Cost:** Total cost of doctoral degree. See note, page 97.

Residency: Indicates whether the school requires on-campus visits for online/DL students

- **None:** The whole program can be taken online/DL.
- **Short-Term:** College requires the students to come to campus, usually for a few weeks or weekends.

Programs and Courses: Undergraduate and graduate degrees offered; courses and certificate programs offered.

Additional Information: Information that does not fit into any other category.

Note: Abbreviations used in these listings include the following: AA (associate of arts); AS (associate of science); BA (bachelor of arts); B.Sc.or BS; (bachelor of science); MA (master of arts); MS (master of science); MBA (master of business administration); MPA (master of public administration); MSW (master of social work); PhD (doctor of philosophy). Total costs are approximate.

If a space is left blank after a topic, information is either not available or not applicable.

SEMESTER CREDIT HOURS AND COST TO COMPLETE DEGREES

Some schools offer quarter hours rather than semester hours. For our purposes, however, all costs have been converted to semester hours in US dollars. One semester hour is approximately 1½ quarter hours. (For example: To convert $100 per quarter hour to its equivalent in semester hours, the equation is: $100 \times \frac{3}{2} = \$150$ per semester hour.)

For the total cost per degree offered, multiply the number of hours needed to graduate by the cost per semester credit hour.

For schools that do not specify the number of hours, you can use the most common requirements by all colleges and universities to estimate the total cost per each degree:

- Associate degree = 64 semester credit hours

- Bachelor's Degree = 128 semester credit hours

- Master's Degree = 36 semester credit hours

- Doctoral Degree = 60 semester credit hours

All costs listed are approximate and usually exclusive of other costs, such as admission, books, software, technology, communication fees, and so on.

Although every effort has been made to provide the most accurate and up-to-date information possible, Web sites, e-mail addresses, costs, and courses are subject to frequent changes. Contact the schools directly to confirm information.

ALGONQUIN COLLEGE

ID	1	**Web Site**	http://www.algonquinc.on.ca/
Type	Private		distance.htm
Established	1958	**E-mail**	distance@algonquinc.on.ca
Regional Accreditation		**Toll-Free**	888-684-4444
Other Valid Accreditation	Yes	**Phone**	613-727-0002
State Approved		**Fax**	613-727-7754
Financial Aid		**Address**	Registrar's Office, Room C150
Total Students			Woodroffe Campus
Online/DL Students			Algonquin College
Undergrad Cr. Hr. Cost	See below		Nepean, Ontario
Grad Cr. Hr. Cost	See below		K2G 1V8
			Canada

☑ **General Courses**	Yes		❑ **Master's**	No
☑ **Certificates**	Yes		Master's Hours	
❑ **Associate**	No		Master's Cost	
Associate Hours			❑ **PhD**	No
Associate Cost			PhD Hours	
❑ **Bachelor's**	No		PhD Cost	
Bachelor's Hours			❑ **Residency**	None
Bachelor's Cost				

Programs and Courses Courses via e-mail and Internet: computer courses, creative writing, entrepreneurship, and technical report writing. Certificates: business studies, information technology fundamentals, palliative care and working with the terminally ill program, and teachers and trainers of adults program. A 30-week online systems support specialist program designed to provide fundamental-to-advanced computer skills and technical knowledge of Microsoft operating systems is available. Cost is $10,900 (Can.).

Additional Information Other course fees vary according to the length and type of course. Students pay a course fee, a material fee, and the cost of the textbook. For current prices, phone 613-727-4723 ext. 7098 or 888-684-4444.

AMERICAN INSTITUTE FOR COMPUTER SCIENCES

ID	2	Web Site	http://www.aics.edu
Type	Private	E-mail	admiss@aics.edu
Established	1988	Toll-Free	800-767-2427
Regional Accreditation		Phone	205-323-6191
Other Valid Accreditation	Yes	Fax	205-328-2229
State Approved	Yes		
Financial Aid	No	Address	American Institute for Computer Sciences
Total Students			
Online/DL Students			2101 Magnolia Avenue, Suite 207
Undergrad Cr. Hr. Cost	$80		Birmingham, AL 35205-2835
Grad Cr. Hr. Cost	$115		

❏ General Courses	No	☑ Master's	Yes
❏ Certificates	No	Master's Hours	36
❏ Associate	No	Master's Cost	$4,140
Associate Hours		❏ PhD	No
Associate Cost		PhD Hours	
☑ Bachelor's	Yes	PhD Cost	
Bachelor's Hours	120	❏ Residency	None
Bachelor's Cost	$9,600		

Programs and Courses Offers BS in computer science, MS in computer science, or BS/MS combination.

Additional Information Credit is awarded for life and work experience and can be transferred from other institutions. Students enrolling in the combination program receive an additional 20 percent off their tuition.

AMERICAN MILITARY UNIVERSITY

ID	3	Web Site	http://www.amunet.edu
Type	Private	E-mail	amugen@amunet.edu
Established	1991	Toll-Free	
Regional Accreditation		Phone	703-330-5398
Other Valid Accreditation	Yes	Fax	703-330-5109
State Approved	Yes		
Financial Aid	No	Address	American Military University
Total Students	1,200		Office of Admissions
Online/DL Students	1,200		9104-P Manassas Drive
Undergrad Cr. Hr. Cost	$133		Manassas Park, VA 20111
Grad Cr. Hr. Cost	$200		

❑ General Courses	No	☑ Master's	Yes
❑ Certificates	No	Master's Hours	36
❑ Associate	No	Master's Cost	$7,200
Associate Hours		❑ PhD	No
Associate Cost		PhD Hours	
☑ Bachelor's	Yes	PhD Cost	
Bachelor's Hours	120	❑ Residency	None
Bachelor's Cost	$15,960		

Programs and Courses To enroll in the bachelor's program, you need an associate or higher degree or at least 45 semester hours from an accredited institution. For the BA, you may select from three majors: military history (American or world), intelligence studies, or military management. For the MA, you may select from seven majors: air warfare, land warfare, naval warfare, unconventional warfare, intelligence studies, defense management, or Civil War studies.

Additional Information The university is planning to offer more scholarships and financial aid programs. The university is accredited by the Distance Education and Training Council (DETC) and is in the process of being accredited regionally. Most of the students are military personnel (60%), but the school is open to students from all backgrounds. Students and professors communicate by e-mail, fax, phone, or mail. AMU presently offers a number of graduate courses via the Internet.

ARIZONA STATE UNIVERSITY

ID	4.	**Web Site**	http://www-distlearn.pp.asu.edu
Type	Public	**E-mail**	distance@asu.edu
Established	1885	**Toll-Free**	
Regional Accreditation	Yes	**Phone**	602-965-6738
Other Valid Accreditation	Yes	**Fax**	
State Approved	Yes		
Financial Aid	No	**Address**	Arizona State University
Total Students	50,000		Distance Learning Technology
Online/DL Students	1,700		PO Box 872904
Undergrad Cr. Hr. Cost	$360		Tempe, AZ 85287-2904
Grad Cr. Hr. Cost			

☑ **General Courses**	Yes		❑ **Master's**	No
❑ **Certificates**	No		Master's Hours	
❑ **Associate**	No		Master's Cost	
Associate Hours			❑ **PhD**	No
Associate Cost			PhD Hours	
❑ **Bachelor's**	No		PhD Cost	
Bachelor's Hours			❑ **Residency**	None
Bachelor's Cost				

Courses and Programs Distance Learning Technology, a division within the College of Extended Education at Arizona State University, uses Instructional Television Fixed Service (ITFS) as well as cable television, public television, satellite, microwave, videotape, CD-ROM, and the Internet to deliver credit courses to students at remote viewing locations. Sixty semester hours of credit may be applied toward a bachelor's degree. Check the Web site for current online course offerings.

Additional Information Residents pay $105 per credit hour.

ATHABASCA UNIVERSITY

ID	5	Web Site	http://www.athabascau.ca
Type	Public	E-mail	auinfo@cs.athabascau.ca
Established	1970	Toll-Free	800-788-9041
Regional Accreditation		Phone	403-675-6100
Other Valid Accreditation	Yes	Fax	403-675-6174
State Approved	Yes		
Financial Aid	Yes	Address	Athabasca University
Total Students			1 University Drive
Online/DL Students	18,384		Athabasca, Alberta
Undergrad Cr. Hr. Cost	See below		T9S 3A3
Grad Cr. Hr. Cost	See below		Canada

☑ General Courses	Yes		☑ Master's	Yes
☑ Certificates	Yes		Master's Hours	Varies
❏ Associate	No		Master's Cost	
Associate Hours			❏ PhD	No
Associate Cost			PhD Hours	
☑ Bachelor's	Yes		PhD Cost	
Bachelor's Hours	Varies		☑ Residency	Short-term
Bachelor's Cost				

Programs and Courses Athabasca University offers full bachelor degree programs in arts, general studies, science, administrative studies, commerce, and nursing. Master's programs are offered in business administration (MBA) and distance education (MDE). A number of certificate programs are offered as well. AU provides courses through numerous and flexible delivery systems (Internet, classroom, teleconference, seminar courses, computer-assisted learning, and printed materials). The school plans to eventually have all courses online.

Additional Information Tuition and fees vary depending on the program and a student's residency status. Contact the school for more details.

AUBURN UNIVERSITY

ID	6	Web Site	http://www.auburn.edu/outreach/dl
Type	Public	E-mail	audl@uce.auburn.edu
Established	1856	Toll-Free	888-844-5300
Regional Accreditation	Yes	Phone	334-844-5300
Other Valid Accreditation	Yes	Fax	334-844-2519
State Approved	Yes		
Financial Aid	No	Address	Auburn University
Total Students	21,000		Graduate Outreach Program
Online/DL Students	400		202 Ramsay Hall
Undergrad Cr. Hr. Cost			Auburn, AL 36849-5336
Grad Cr. Hr. Cost	See below		

☑ General Courses	Yes	☑ Master's	Yes
❑ Certificates	No	Master's Hours	Varies
❑ Associate	No	Master's Cost	
Associate Hours		☑ PhD	Yes
Associate Cost		PhD Hours	Varies
❑ Bachelor's	No	PhD Cost	
Bachelor's Hours		☑ Residency	Short-term
Bachelor's Cost			

Programs and Courses Graduate: MBA; master's and PhD degrees in aerospace engineering, chemical engineering, civil engineering, computer science and engineering, industrial and systems engineering, materials engineering, and mechanical engineering. The PhD programs require the student to complete three consecutive quarters on campus. A number of independent learning courses are available online.

Additional Information Tuition for engineering courses is $195 per credit hour; MBA courses are $225 per credit hour. Other fees apply. *U.S. News and World Report* ranked Auburn as the 27th best value of national universities in the United States; *Kiplinger's Personal Finance Magazine* rated Auburn among the top 20 public universities in the United States. The school uses videotape and e-mail for course delivery.

BELLEVUE UNIVERSITY

ID	7	Web Site	http://bruins.bellevue.edu/
Type	Private		Online/intro.htm
Established	1966	E-mail	cbv@scholars.bellevue.edu
Regional Accreditation	Yes	Toll-Free	800-756-7920
Other Valid Accreditation	Yes	Phone	402-291-8100
State Approved	Yes	Fax	
Financial Aid	Yes		
Total Students	2,928	Address	Bellevue University
Online/DL Students	70		Online Admission
Undergrad Cr. Hr. Cost	$250		1000 Galvin Road South
Grad Cr. Hr. Cost	$275		Bellevue, NE 68005

❑ General Courses	No	☑ Master's	Yes
❑ Certificates	No	Master's Hours	32
❑ Associate	No	Master's Cost	$8,800
Associate Hours		❑ PhD	No
Associate Cost		PhD Hours	
☑ Bachelor's	Yes	PhD Cost	
Bachelor's Hours	36	❑ Residency	None
Bachelor's Cost	$9,000		

Programs and Courses Undergraduate: accelerated BS in management, management information systems, international business management, and criminal justice administration. Graduate: MBA or MA in leadership.

Additional Information You must have at least 60 credit hours from an accredited institution or an accredited associate degree to qualify for admission to the bachelor's degree program. Online undergraduate programs require a total of 127 credit hours including the 36-hour major that must be completed through Bellevue.

BEMIDJI STATE UNIVERSITY

ID	8	**Web Site**	http://www.bemidji.msus.edu
Type	Public	**E-mail**	cel@vax1.bemidji.msus.edu
Established	1973	**Toll-Free**	800-475-2001
Regional Accreditation	Yes	**Phone**	218-755-2068
Other Valid Accreditation	Yes	**Fax**	
State Approved	Yes		
Financial Aid	Yes	**Address**	Bemidji State University
Total Students	5,400		Center for Extended Learning
Online/DL Students	1,500		1500 Birchmont Drive NE
Undergrad Cr. Hr. Cost	$194		Bemidji, MN 56601-2699
Grad Cr. Hr. Cost			

☑ **General Courses**	Yes	❑ **Master's**	No
☑ **Certificates**	Yes	Master's Hours	
☑ **Associate**	Yes	Master's Cost	
Associate Hours	64	❑ **PhD**	No
Associate Cost	$12,416	PhD Hours	
☑ **Bachelor's**	Yes	PhD Cost	
Bachelor's Hours	128	☑ **Residency**	Short-term
Bachelor's Cost	$24,832		

Programs and Courses Liberal studies (AA), criminal justice (AS). Undergraduate: criminal justice (BS), social studies (BA), history (BA). Courses are delivered via audio cassette, video tape, interactive TV, and the Internet. The school is in the process of modifying more courses for delivery using the Internet. Contact the Center for Extended Learning for more information.

Additional Information Courses are also offered in fields such as anthropology, chemistry, English, geography, health, music, philosophy, physical education, political science, psychology, science, social work, and sociology. Courses available will vary from term to term. The university is in the process of converting from quarter to semester credit hour system.

BENJAMIN FRANKLIN INSTITUTE
OF GLOBAL EDUCATION

ID	9	Web Site	http://www.bfranklin.edu
Type	Private	E-mail	
Established	1990	Toll-Free	
Regional Accreditation		Phone	619-680-3950
Other Valid Accreditation		Fax	619-270-2667
State Approved	Yes		
Financial Aid	No	Address	Benjamin Franklin Institute of
Total Students			Global Education
Online/DL Students			4241 Jutland Avenue, Suite 2000
Undergrad Cr. Hr. Cost			San Diego, CA 92117
Grad Cr. Hr. Cost			

☑ General Courses	Yes		☑ Master's	Yes
☑ Certificates	Yes		Master's Hours	
☑ Associate	Yes		Master's Cost	
Associate Hours			☑ PhD	Yes
Associate Cost			PhD Hours	
☑ Bachelor's	Yes		PhD Cost	
Bachelor's Hours			☐ Residency	None
Bachelor's Cost				

Programs and Courses This site provides links to distance education schools and resources that list more than 30,000 courses from more than 1,000 accredited institutions worldwide. Some of these courses use the Internet as a media of delivery. Contact the institution for more details.

Additional Information The Institute was founded in Europe to help motivated Americans enter the international arena through teach and work programs offered globally. It trains, recruits, and sends overseas professionals who wish to teach English and other subjects. Courses can be designed to match the student's needs.

BOISE STATE UNIVERSITY

ID	10	**Web Site**	http://coe.idbsu.edu/coeng/dep/
Type	Public		ipt/iptde.htm
Established	1932	**E-mail**	bsu-ipt@micron.net
Regional Accreditation	Yes	**Toll-Free**	800-824-7017
Other Valid Accreditation	Yes	**Phone**	208-385-4457
State Approved	Yes	**Fax**	208-342-1970
Financial Aid	Yes	**Address**	IPT Department, ET-338
Total Students	4,200		College of Engineering
Online/DL Students	100		Boise State University
Undergrad Cr. Hr. Cost			1910 University Drive
Grad Cr. Hr. Cost	$315		Boise, ID 83725

☑ **General Courses**	Yes		☑ **Master's**	Yes
☐ **Certificates**	No		Master's Hours	36
☐ **Associate**	No		Master's Cost	$11,340
Associate Hours			☐ **PhD**	No
Associate Cost			PhD Hours	
☐ **Bachelor's**	No		PhD Cost	
Bachelor's Hours			☐ **Residency**	None
Bachelor's Cost				

Programs and Courses The university offers a master's of science degree in instructional and performance technology, using asynchronous computer conferencing as its primary vehicle for delivering instruction. Other fees apply.

Additional Information Select courses are offered via the Internet each semester through the Department of Continuing Education. Call (208) 385-1709 or visit http://www.idbsu.edu/conted/ for a current list of courses.

BREVARD COMMUNITY COLLEGE

ID	11	Web Site	http://www.brevard.cc.fl.us/distlrn
Type	Public	E-mail	info@a1.brevard.cc.fl.us
Established	1960	Toll-Free	
Regional Accreditation	Yes	Phone	407-632-1111
Other Valid Accreditation	Yes	Fax	
State Approved	Yes		
Financial Aid	Yes	Address	Brevard Community College
Total Students	42,000		1519 Clearlake Road
Online/DL Students	1,200		Cocoa, FL 32922
Undergrad Cr. Hr. Cost	$140		
Grad Cr. Hr. Cost			

☑ General Courses	Yes	❑ Master's	No
❑ Certificates	No	Master's Hours	
☑ Associate	Yes	Master's Cost	
Associate Hours	60	❑ PhD	No
Associate Cost	$8,400	PhD Hours	
❑ Bachelor's	No	PhD Cost	
Bachelor's Hours		❑ Residency	None
Bachelor's Cost			

Programs and Courses BCC's virtual campus provides online courses applicable to an associate in arts degree and an associate in science degree in legal assisting. Other select courses are available online. The school is currently reorganizing aspects of its online courses. Contact an adviser for more information.

Additional Information Residents pay $44 per credit hour for online courses. BCC's virtual campus provides online instruction and learner supported services, including access to an AA degree program and 10 AS degree programs. BCC offers a comprehensive tele-course program that enrolls over 3,500 students annually through more than 90 tele-courses. BCC students can earn an AA degree entirely through telecourses.

BUCKS COUNTY COMMUNITY COLLEGE

ID	12	**Web Site**	http://www.bucks.edu
Type	Public	**E-mail**	learning@bucks.edu
Established	1964	**Toll-Free**	
Regional Accreditation	Yes	**Phone**	215-968-8052
Other Valid Accreditation	Yes	**Fax**	215-968-8148
State Approved	Yes		
Financial Aid	Yes	**Address**	Bucks County Community College
Total Students	10,434		Office of Distance Learning
Online/DL Students			434 Swamp Road
Undergrad Cr. Hr. Cost	$213		Newtown, PA 18940
Grad Cr. Hr. Cost			

☑ **General Courses**	Yes		❑ **Master's**	No
❑ **Certificates**	No		Master's Hours	
☑ **Associate**	Yes		Master's Cost	
Associate Hours	60		❑ **PhD**	No
Associate Cost	$12,780		PhD Hours	
❑ **Bachelor's**	No		PhD Cost	
Bachelor's Hours			☑ **Residency**	Short-term
Bachelor's Cost				

Programs and Courses More than 60 courses in almost every program of study are available through BCCC's distance learning program. Associate degrees: liberal arts (general emphasis), business administration, and management/marketing. Degree requirements and distance learning course availability for completion of these programs can be obtained from college Web site.

Additional Information Resident students pay lower tuition rates; other fees apply. Technologies used in delivering education: mail, videotapes, Internet, telephone, voice mail, fax, and e-mail in addition to Alta Vista Forum, a Web-based communication tool used for sharing information, holding online discussions, and collaborating with classmates.

CALIFORNIA COLLEGE FOR HEALTH SCIENCES

ID	13	Web Site	http://www.cchs.edu
Type	Private	E-mail	ahp@cchs.edu
Established	1978	Toll-Free	800-221-7374
Regional Accreditation		Phone	619-477-4800
Other Valid Accreditation	Yes	Fax	619-477-4360
State Approved	Yes		
Financial Aid	No	Address	California College for Health
Total Students	7,030		Sciences
Online/DL Students	7,000		222 West 24th Street
Undergrad Cr. Hr. Cost	$100		National City, CA 91950
Grad Cr. Hr. Cost	$100		

☑ General Courses	Yes	☑ Master's	Yes
☑ Certificates	Yes	Master's Hours	36
☑ Associate	Yes	Master's Cost	$3,600
Associate Hours	60	❑ PhD	No
Associate Cost	Varies	PhD Hours	
☑ Bachelor's	Yes	PhD Cost	
Bachelor's Hours	120	❑ Residency	None
Bachelor's Cost	$12,000		

Programs and Courses The college offers a variety of degree and continuing education programs in a number of health and human service disciplines. Bachelor's degree in health services with emphasis in management or respiratory care. AS degrees in allied health and business, medical transcription, EEG technology, early childhood education, respiratory technology, and respiratory therapy. Vocational/technical programs, corporate training, and continuing education courses. Master's of science in community health administration and wellness promotion.

Additional Information The college is accredited by the Distance Education and Training Council (DETC) in Washington, DC. Additional fees apply. No financial aid is available, but the college offers flexible payment plans.

CALIFORNIA INSTITUTE OF INTEGRAL STUDIES

ID	14	Web Site	http://www.ciis.edu
Type	Private	E-mail	info@ciis.edu
Established	1968	Toll-Free	
Regional Accreditation	Yes	Phone	415-674-5500
Other Valid Accreditation	Yes	Fax	
State Approved	Yes		
Financial Aid	Yes	Address	California Institute of Integral
Total Students	1,200		Studies
Online/DL Students			9 Peter Yorke Way
Undergrad Cr. Hr. Cost			San Francisco, CA 94109
Grad Cr. Hr. Cost	See below		

☑ General Courses	Yes	☐ Master's	No
☐ Certificates	No	Master's Hours	
☐ Associate	No	Master's Cost	
Associate Hours		☑ PhD	Yes
Associate Cost		PhD Hours	See below
☐ Bachelor's	No	PhD Cost	$31,500
Bachelor's Hours		☑ Residency	Short-term
Bachelor's Cost			

Programs and Courses A PhD in humanities with a concentration in transformative learning and change is available online. Other online elective courses are available each quarter. The PhD requires 90 quarter units, and tuition is $350 per unit. Other fees apply.

CALIFORNIA NATIONAL UNIVERSITY

ID	15	Web Site	http://www.cnuas.edu
Type	Private	E-mail	cnuadms@mail.cnuas.edu
Established	1993	Toll-Free	800-782-2422
Regional Accreditation		Phone	
Other Valid Accreditation	Yes	Fax	
State Approved	Yes		
Financial Aid	No	Address	California National University
Total Students			16909 Parthenia Street
Online/DL Students	200		North Hills, CA 91343
Undergrad Cr. Hr. Cost	$195		
Grad Cr. Hr. Cost	$210		

☑ General Courses	Yes		☑ Master's	Yes
❑ Certificates	No		Master's Hours	36
❑ Associate	No		Master's Cost	$7,560
Associate Hours			❑ PhD	No
Associate Cost			PhD Hours	
☑ Bachelor's	Yes		PhD Cost	
Bachelor's Hours	120		❑ Residency	None
Bachelor's Cost	$23,400			

Programs and Courses Bachelor of quality assurance science; bachelor of computer science; business administration (BS, MS); engineering (BS, MS); and master of human resource management. The required number of hours listed above are estimates.

Additional Information The school does not offer financial aid but it provides flexible payment plans. Study materials and software are shipped to students by UPS. Students can communicate with their instructors using phone, fax, Web forum, and e-mail. The school may award credit for life-related work experience. Accreditation: The school is accredited by the Distance Education and Training Council (DETC).

CALIFORNIA STATE UNIVERSITY– DOMINGUEZ HILLS

ID	16	**Web Site**	http://www.csudh.edu/
Type	Public		dominguezonline
Established	1960	**E-mail**	exted@dhvx20.csudh.edu
Regional Accreditation	Yes	**Toll-Free**	
Other Valid Accreditation	Yes	**Phone**	310-243-2288
State Approved	Yes	**Fax**	310-516-3971
Financial Aid	No	**Address**	SCC B141
Total Students	447		CSU Dominguez Hills
Online/DL Students	3,200		The Office of Extended Education
Undergrad Cr. Hr. Cost	See below		1000 East Victoria Street
Grad Cr. Hr. Cost	See below		Carson, CA 90747

☑ **General Courses**	Yes	☑ **Master's**	Yes
☑ **Certificates**	Yes	Master's Hours	Varies
❏ **Associate**	No	Master's Cost	
Associate Hours		❏ **PhD**	No
Associate Cost		PhD Hours	
☑ **Bachelor's**	Yes	PhD Cost	
Bachelor's Hours	Varies	☑ **Residency**	Short-term
Bachelor's Cost			

Programs and Courses Graduate: quality assurance (MS); humanities (MA); behavioral science (MA); MBA. Undergraduate: interdisciplinary studies (BA); nursing (BS). Certificates: production and inventory control, purchasing. Tuition varies by program.

Additional Information In 1997 the university was voted by *Forbes* magazine as one of the nation's top 20 cyber universities. CSUDH uses TV broadcasting, videotapes, and the Internet to deliver the distance learning programs.

CALIFORNIA STATE UNIVERSITY–LONG BEACH

ID	17	**Web Site**	http://www.uces.csulb.edu
Type	Public	**E-mail**	ideas@uces.csulb.edu
Established	1947	**Toll-Free**	(800) 963-2250
Regional Accreditation	Yes	**Phone**	(562) 985-8447
Other Valid Accreditation	Yes	**Fax**	(562) 985-8449
State Approved	Yes	**Address**	University College and Extension
Financial Aid	No		Services, CSULB
Total Students			6300 State University Drive, Suite
Online/DL Students			104
Undergrad Cr. Hr. Cost	See below		Long Beach, CA 90815
Grad Cr. Hr. Cost			Attn: IDEAS

☑ **General Courses**	Yes		❏ **Master's**	No
❏ **Certificates**	No		Master's Hours	
❏ **Associate**	No		Master's Cost	
Associate Hours			❏ **PhD**	No
Associate Cost			PhD Hours	
❏ **Bachelor's**	No		PhD Cost	
Bachelor's Hours			❏ **Residency**	None
Bachelor's Cost				

Programs and Courses Integrated Distance Education for Adult Students (IDEAS) offers selected courses through the World Wide Web. With a computer, a modem, and Internet connectivity, distance learners have access to the same expert faculty and quality instruction that characterize the on-campus courses. Three-credit courses currently cost $540. Other distance learning options are available.

CALIFORNIA STATE UNIVERSITY–NORTHRIDGE

ID	18	**Web Site**	http://www.csun.edu
Type	Public	**E-mail**	exl@huey.csun.edu
Established	1857	**Toll-Free**	(800) 677-2355
Regional Accreditation	Yes	**Phone**	(818) 677-2270
Other Valid Accreditation	Yes	**Fax**	
State Approved	Yes		
Financial Aid	No	**Address**	California State University—
Total Students	26,000		Northridge
Online/DL Students	5,000		Office of Extended Learning
Undergrad Cr. Hr. Cost	Varies		18111 Nordhoff Street
Grad Cr. Hr. Cost	Varies		Northridge, CA 91330-8324

☑ **General Courses**	Yes		☑ **Master's**	Yes
☑ **Certificates**	Yes		Master's Hours	
❑ **Associate**	No		Master's Cost	
Associate Hours			❑ **PhD**	No
Associate Cost			PhD Hours	
❑ **Bachelor's**	No		PhD Cost	
Bachelor's Hours			☑ **Residency**	Short-term
Bachelor's Cost				

Programs and Courses An electronic network allows students in California to complete under-graduate prerequisites, obtain teacher credentialing, or take courses in communication disorders and sciences, engineering and computer science, and special education. A master's online degree program in speech pathology is being developed. General online courses available in art, speech communication, English, history, computer science, health science, math, and more.

Additional Information CSUN is in the top 10% nationally in terms of size. Main vehicle of educational delivery is satellite and TV broadcasting throughout California. For the college connection near you, call 800-777-6463.

CHAMPLAIN COLLEGE

ID	19	**Web Site**	http://www.champlain.edu
Type	Private	**E-mail**	online@champlain.edu
Established	1878	**Toll-Free**	888-545-3459
Regional Accreditation	Yes	**Phone**	
Other Valid Accreditation	Yes	**Fax**	
State Approved	Yes		
Financial Aid	Yes	**Address**	Champlain College Online
Total Students			Champlain College
Online/DL Students			163 South Willard Street
Undergrad Cr. Hr. Cost	$295		Burlington, VT 05402-0670
Grad Cr. Hr. Cost			

☑ **General Courses**	Yes	❑ **Master's**	No
☑ **Certificates**	Yes	Master's Hours	
☑ **Associate**	Yes	Master's Cost	
Associate Hours	60	❑ **PhD**	No
Associate Cost	$17,700	PhD Hours	
☑ **Bachelor's**	Yes	PhD Cost	
Bachelor's Hours	120	❑ **Residency**	None
Bachelor's Cost	$35,400		

Programs and Courses Certificates and associate degrees: accounting, business, computer programming, hotel-restaurant management, management, travel and tourism. Bachelor's degrees: liberal studies, computer programming, and business.

Additional Information Offers a free course to evaluate their online program. Champlain College offers completion baccalaureate (BS) degrees in Israel through a contractual agreement with the Israeli College of Business Administration under I.S.E. Modem, an Israeli public company. Classes are held at five different locations: Tel Aviv, Haifa, Jerusalem, Beer-sheba, and Ashdod.

CHRISTOPHER NEWPORT UNIVERSITY

ID	20	**Web Site**	http://cnuonline.cnu.edu
Type	Public	**E-mail**	online@cnu.edu
Established	1960	**Toll-Free**	800-333-4268
Regional Accreditation	Yes	**Phone**	757-594-7015
Other Valid Accreditation	Yes	**Fax**	
State Approved	Yes		
Financial Aid	No	**Address**	Christopher Newport University
Total Students	4,500		Dean of Admissions
Online/DL Students	500		Newport News, VA 23606-2998
Undergrad Cr. Hr. Cost	$338		
Grad Cr. Hr. Cost			

☑ **General Courses**	Yes	☐ **Master's**	No
☐ **Certificates**	No	Master's Hours	
☐ **Associate**	No	Master's Cost	
Associate Hours		☐ **PhD**	No
Associate Cost		PhD Hours	
☑ **Bachelor's**	Yes	PhD Cost	
Bachelor's Hours	128	☐ **Residency**	None
Bachelor's Cost	$43,264		

Programs and Courses Undergraduate: BS in governmental administration with a concentration in criminal justice administration, public management, or international administration; BA in philosophy and religious studies. More degrees are being added.

Additional Information Cost per credit hour for state residents is $143.

CITY UNIVERSITY

ID	21	**Web Site**	http://www.cityu.edu
Type	Private	**E-mail**	info@cityu.edu
Established	1973	**Toll-Free**	800-426-5596
Regional Accreditation	Yes	**Phone**	425-637-1010
Other Valid Accreditation	Yes	**Fax**	425-277-2437
State Approved	Yes		
Financial Aid	Yes	**Address**	City University
Total Students			Distance Learning Office
Online/DL Students	14,000		919 SW Grady Way
Undergrad Cr. Hr. Cost	$225		Renton, WA 98055
Grad Cr. Hr. Cost	$402		

☑ **General Courses**	Yes	☑ **Master's**	Yes
☑ **Certificates**	Yes	Master's Hours	30
☑ **Associate**	Yes	Master's Cost	$12,060
Associate Hours	60	❏ **PhD**	No
Associate Cost	$13,500	PhD Hours	
☑ **Bachelor's**	Yes	PhD Cost	
Bachelor's Hours	120	❏ **Residency**	None
Bachelor's Cost	$27,000		

Programs and Courses City University offers more than 50 programs at the undergraduate and graduate levels. The school offers courses on-site, but the majority of the programs are available through distance learning, including several courses on the Web. Some of the available programs are undergraduate and graduate certificates; BS in accounting, marketing, or general studies; BA with an emphasis in humanities, social sciences, or commerce; MBA; MPA; MEd; master of management; master of project managment.

Additional Information City University's two dozen instructional sites (in the West Coast of the United States, Europe, and the Middle East) serve more than 14,000 students worldwide. The university's MBA and MEd programs are among the largest in the nation. Additional fees apply.

CLARKSON COLLEGE

ID	22	**Web Site**	http://www.clarksoncollege.edu
Type	Private	**E-mail**	admiss@clrkcol.crhsnet.edu
Established	1883	**Toll-Free**	800-647-5500
Regional Accreditation	Yes	**Phone**	402-552-3037
Other Valid Accreditation	Yes	**Fax**	402-552-6057
State Approved	Yes		
Financial Aid	Yes	**Address**	Clarkson College
Total Students	700		101 South 42nd Street
Online/DL Students	210		Omaha, NE 68131-2739
Undergrad Cr. Hr. Cost	$272		
Grad Cr. Hr. Cost	$314		

☑ **General Courses**	Yes	☑ **Master's**	Yes
☐ **Certificates**	No	Master's Hours	36
☐ **Associate**	No	Master's Cost	$11,304
Associate Hours		☐ **PhD**	No
Associate Cost		PhD Hours	
☑ **Bachelor's**	Yes	PhD Cost	
Bachelor's Hours	128	☑ **Residency**	Short-term
Bachelor's Cost	$34,816		

Programs and Courses Clarkson offers undergraduate and graduate degrees in the health science field. Courses are organized into three 16-week semesters (fall, spring, and summer). Undergraduate: medical imaging (BS), business (BS), RN to BSN program. Graduate: nursing (MS), health services management (MS).

Additional Information Students can receive credit for past military or work experience.

THE COLLEGE OF ST. SCHOLASTICA

ID	23	**Web Site**	http://www.css.edu
Type	Private	**E-mail**	admissions@css.edu
Established	1912	**Toll-Free**	800-888-8796
Regional Accreditation	Yes	**Phone**	218-723-6108
Other Valid Accreditation	Yes	**Fax**	
State Approved	Yes		
Financial Aid	Yes	**Address**	Master of Education Via
Total Students	1,840		Distance Learning
Online/DL Students	300		The College of St. Scholastica
Undergrad Cr. Hr. Cost			1200 Kenwood Avenue
Grad Cr. Hr. Cost	See below		Duluth, MN 55811-4199

☑ **General Courses**	Yes	☑ **Master's**	Yes
❑ **Certificates**	No	**Master's Hours**	48
❑ **Associate**	No	**Master's Cost**	
Associate Hours		❑ **PhD**	No
Associate Cost		**PhD Hours**	
❑ **Bachelor's**	No	**PhD Cost**	
Bachelor's Hours		☑ **Residency**	Short-term
Bachelor's Cost			

Programs and Courses Graduate: master of education. The school is currently developing Web-based courses. Contact the school for tuition rates.

Additional Information Lectures are videotaped and mailed to students along with study materials. Students can communicate with their instructors using phone, fax, and e-mail. In 1995, *U.S. News and World Report* ranked the college as being one of the top 10 "best values" among Midwest regional universities.

COLORADO STATE UNIVERSITY

ID	24	Web Site	http://www.colostate.edu/Depts/CE
Type	Public	E-mail	info@learn.colostate.edu
Established	1800	Toll-Free	800-525-4950
Regional Accreditation	Yes	Phone	970-491-5288
Other Valid Accreditation	Yes	Fax	970- 491-7885
State Approved	Yes		
Financial Aid	Yes	Address	Continuing Education SURGE
Total Students	24,000		Program
Online/DL Students	700		Spruce Hall
Undergrad Cr. Hr. Cost	$364		Fort Collins, CO 80523-1040
Grad Cr. Hr. Cost	$364		

☑ General Courses	Yes	☑ Master's	Yes
☑ Certificates	Yes	Master's Hours	30–42
❑ Associate	No	Master's Cost	Varies
Associate Hours		☑ PhD	Yes
Associate Cost		PhD Hours	Varies
☑ Bachelor's	Yes	PhD Cost	Varies
Bachelor's Hours	128	☑ Residency	Short-term
Bachelor's Cost	$46,592		

Programs and Courses The SURGE program offers bioresource and agricultural engineering (MS, PhD); MBA; chemical engineering (MS, PhD); civil engineering (MS, PhD); computer science (2nd BS, MS); electrical engineering (MS, PhD); vocational education (MEd); industrial engineering (MS, PhD); business administration (MS); mechanical engineering (MS, PhD); statistics (MS); systems engineering and optimization program (MS, PhD). Classes are videotaped and sent to students by UPS. Students communicate with instructors by e-mail, fax, and mail.

Additional Information For PhDs, a minimum of 72 semester credits beyond the baccalaureate is required. Some doctorate programs require short-term residency. SURGE is available only in the United States, Canada, and to individuals with APO or FPO addresses. The Distance Education Department is currently in the process of developing online credit courses. Call for availability.

DAKOTA STATE UNIVERSITY

ID	25	Web Site	http://www.dsu.edu
Type	Public	E-mail	dsuinfo@columbia.dsu.edu
Established	1881	Toll-Free	800-641-4309
Regional Accreditation	Yes	Phone	605-256-5049
Other Valid Accreditation	Yes	Fax	605-256-5208
State Approved	Yes		
Financial Aid	No	Address	Dakota State University
Total Students	1300		Office of Distance Education
Online/DL Students	384		201A Karl E. Mundt Library
Undergrad Cr. Hr. Cost	$156		Madison, SD 57042
Grad Cr. Hr. Cost	$182		

☑ General Courses	Yes	❑ Master's	No	
❑ Certificates	No	Master's Hours		
❑ Associate	No	Master's Cost		
Associate Hours		❑ PhD	No	
Associate Cost		PhD Hours		
❑ Bachelor's	No	PhD Cost		
Bachelor's Hours		❑ Residency	None	
Bachelor's Cost				

Programs and Courses DSU offers a variety of both graduate and undergraduate courses via the Internet to students throughout the world. The distance education program has expanded to include Internet courses in health information administration.

Additional Information Tuition and fees for South Dakota residents: undergraduate, $129 per credit hour; graduate, $158 per credit hour.

DUKE UNIVERSITY

ID	26	**Web Site**	http://www.fuqua.duke.edu
Type	Private	**E-mail**	fuqua-gemba@mail.duke.edu
Established	1924	**Toll-Free**	800-372-3932
Regional Accreditation	Yes	**Phone**	919-660-7804
Other Valid Accreditation	Yes	**Fax**	919-660-8044
State Approved	Yes		
Financial Aid	Yes	**Address**	The Fuqua School of Business
Total Students			Duke University
Online/DL Students	1,000		EMBA Programs
Undergrad Cr. Hr. Cost			Box 90127
Grad Cr. Hr. Cost	See below		Durham, NC 27708-0127

❑ **General Courses**	No	☑ **Master's**	Yes
❑ **Certificates**	No	Master's Hours	See below
❑ **Associate**	No	Master's Cost	$85,800
Associate Hours		❑ **PhD**	No
Associate Cost		PhD Hours	
❑ **Bachelor's**	No	PhD Cost	
Bachelor's Hours		☑ **Residency**	Short-term
Bachelor's Cost			

Programs and Courses The Global Executive MBA (GEMBA) is an innovative master's degree program for executives and high-potential managers of global corporations offered by The Fuqua School of Business. The program consists of 15 courses grouped into five modules over a 19-month period. Students spend a total of 11 weeks in residential classes at various program sites around the world. Fuqua faculty deliver the balance of the instruction using interactive, distance-education technology

Additional Information For the class entering May 1999, tuition is $85,800. The tuition is fixed for each entering class. Tuition includes a laptop computer, portable printer, books and other class materials, and lodging and meals while at the five sites of residential sessions. The tuition does not include travel to and from the various sites.

EASTERN OREGON UNIVERSITY

ID	27	Web Site	http://www.eou.edu/dep
Type	Public	E-mail	jhart@eosc.osshe.edu
Established	1808	Toll-Free	800-544-2195
Regional Accreditation	Yes	Phone	541-962-3378
Other Valid Accreditation	Yes	Fax	541-962-3627
State Approved	Yes		
Financial Aid	Yes	Address	Eastern Oregon University
Total Students	2,000		Division of Extended Programs
Online/DL Students	700		1410 "L" Avenue
Undergrad Cr. Hr. Cost	Varies		La Grande, OR 97850
Grad Cr. Hr. Cost	Varies		

☑ General Courses	Yes	❑ Master's	No
❑ Certificates	No	Master's Hours	
☑ Associate	Yes	Master's Cost	
Associate Hours		❑ PhD	No
Associate Cost		PhD Hours	
☑ Bachelor's	Yes	PhD Cost	
Bachelor's Hours		❑ Residency	None
Bachelor's Cost			

Programs and Courses AS in office administration. Undergraduate: BA/BS in liberal studies; business/economics; or philosophy, politics, and economics. The university also offers seven Web-based courses (in business, political science, and screenwriting) and sixty-one computer conferencing courses (from art to writing) that are open to students anywhere who can access the courses via the Internet. Contact the school for tuition rates.

ELECTRONIC UNIVERSITY NETWORK

ID	28	**Web Site**	http://www.wcc-eun.com
Type	Private	**E-mail**	EUNLearn@aol.com
Established	1983	**Toll-Free**	800-225-3276
Regional Accreditation	Yes	**Phone**	541-482-5871
Other Valid Accreditation	Yes	**Fax**	541-482-7544
State Approved	Yes		
Financial Aid	Yes	**Address**	Electronic University Network
Total Students			1977 Colestin Road
Online/DL Students			Hombrook, CA 96044
Undergrad Cr. Hr. Cost			
Grad Cr. Hr. Cost			

☑ **General Courses**	Yes		☑ **Master's**	Yes
☑ **Certificates**	Yes		Master's Hours	
☑ **Associate**	Yes		Master's Cost	
Associate Hours			☑ **PhD**	Yes
Associate Cost			PhD Hours	
☑ **Bachelor's**	Yes		PhD Cost	
Bachelor's Hours			☑ **Residency**	Varies
Bachelor's Cost				

Programs and Courses EUN is a good source of distance/online higher education. EUN does not offer courses itself, but it does registration, admissions, and counseling for a number of accredited colleges and universities offering online education. Cost, degrees, and financial aid vary from one school to another.

Additional Information EUN works with the online and distance learning programs for the following colleges and universities (32 degrees and 400 courses): Brevard Community College, Rogers University—Claremore, City University, Michigan State University, Heriot-Watt University, Salve Regina University, Walden University, University of Wisconsin—Stout, Norwich University, and California Institute of Integral Studies.

EMBRY-RIDDLE AERONAUTICAL UNIVERSITY

ID	29	Web Site	http://ec.db.erau.edu
Type	Private	E-mail	indstudy@cts.db.erau.edu
Established	1926	Toll-Free	800-522-6787
Regional Accreditation	Yes	Phone	904-226-6263
Other Valid Accreditation	Yes	Fax	
State Approved	Yes	Address	Extended Campus
Financial Aid	No		Embry-Riddle Aeronautical
Total Students	17,000		University
Online/DL Students	2,000		600 South Clyde Morris Boulevard
Undergrad Cr. Hr. Cost	$130		Daytona Beach, FL 32114
Grad Cr. Hr. Cost	$280		

❏ General Courses	No	☑ Master's	Yes
❏ Certificates	No	Master's Hours	
☑ Associate	Yes	Master's Cost	
Associate Hours		❏ PhD	No
Associate Cost		PhD Hours	
☑ Bachelor's	Yes	PhD Cost	
Bachelor's Hours		☑ Residency	Short-term
Bachelor's Cost			

Programs and Courses Distance learning classes support requirements for awarding the following degrees: associate in science and bachelor of science in professional aeronautics, the associate in science in aviation business administration, and the bachelor of science in management of technical operations. A master of aeronautical science degree is available with aviation/aerospace specialization in management, operations, or safety systems.

Additional Information Embry-Riddle Aeronautical University is the world's oldest, largest, and most prestigious university specializing in the field of aviation and aerospace.

EMPORIA STATE UNIVERSITY

ID	30	**Web Site**	http://www.emporia.edu
Type	Public	**E-mail**	conted@esumail.emporia.edu
Established	1863	**Toll-Free**	
Regional Accreditation	Yes	**Phone**	316-341-5385
Other Valid Accreditation	Yes	**Fax**	316-341-5744
State Approved	Yes		
Financial Aid	No	**Address**	Emporia State University
Total Students	5,800		Office of Continuing Education
Online/DL Students			1200 Commercial, Box 4052
Undergrad Cr. Hr. Cost	$72		Emporia, KS 66801
Grad Cr. Hr. Cost	$102		

☑ **General Courses**	Yes	☐ **Master's**	No
☐ **Certificates**	No	Master's Hours	
☐ **Associate**	No	Master's Cost	
Associate Hours		☐ **PhD**	No
Associate Cost		PhD Hours	
☐ **Bachelor's**	No	PhD Cost	
Bachelor's Hours		☐ **Residency**	None
Bachelor's Cost			

Programs and Courses   The university offers online courses in biological sciences, communication and theater arts, computer science, English, health and physical education, instructional design and technology, physical sciences, and library and information management.

Additional Information   Degree programs offered beginning Fall 1998; contact the school for more information.

FLORIDA STATE UNIVERSITY

ID	31	**Web Site**	http://idl.fsu.edu
Type	Public	**E-mail**	idl-info@lsi.fsu.edu
Established		**Toll-Free**	
Regional Accreditation	Yes	**Phone**	904-644-3614
Other Valid Accreditation	Yes	**Fax**	904-644-2589
State Approved	Yes		
Financial Aid	Yes	**Address**	Florida State University
Total Students			Interactive Distance Learning
Online/DL Students			109 Westcott
Undergrad Cr. Hr. Cost	See below		Tallahassee, FL 32306-2027
Grad Cr. Hr. Cost			

☑ **General Courses**	Yes	☑ **Master's**	Yes
❑ **Certificates**	No	**Master's Hours**	36
❑ **Associate**	No	**Master's Cost**	
Associate Hours		❑ **PhD**	No
Associate Cost		**PhD Hours**	
☑ **Bachelor's**	Yes	**PhD Cost**	
Bachelor's Hours	120	☑ **Residency**	Short-term
Bachelor's Cost			

Programs and Courses Currently under development for Web-based delivery are the following degree programs: bachelor's degree in criminology and criminal justice, master's degree in information studies, and master's degree in open and distance learning (a collaborative venture with the Open University of the United Kingdom). Contact the school for more information on the status of the above programs. Fees for interactive distance learning, off-campus courses vary by course and program.

Additional Information The university is in the process of developing more distance and online courses and degree programs.

THE GRADUATE SCHOOL OF AMERICA

ID	32	**Web Site**	http://www.tgsa.com
Type	Private	**E-mail**	tgsainfo@tgsa.edu
Established	1993	**Toll-Free**	800-987-1133
Regional Accreditation	Yes	**Phone**	612-339-8650
Other Valid Accreditation	Yes	**Fax**	
State Approved	Yes		
Financial Aid	Yes	**Address**	The Graduate School of America
Total Students	322		330 2nd Avenue South, Suite 550
Online/DL Students	322		Minneapolis, MN 55401
Undergrad Cr. Hr. Cost			
Grad Cr. Hr. Cost	See below		

❑ **General Courses**	No	☑ **Master's**	Yes
❑ **Certificates**	No	Master's Hours	32
❑ **Associate**	No	Master's Cost	
Associate Hours		☑ **PhD**	Yes
Associate Cost		PhD Hours	80
❑ **Bachelor's**	No	PhD Cost	
Bachelor's Hours		☑ **Residency**	Short-term
Bachelor's Cost			

Programs and Courses TGSA offers MS degrees (48 quarter credits) in education, human services (counseling emphasis), organization and management, and organization and management (communications technology). PhD degrees (120 quarter credits) in education, education (school age care), human services, organization and management, organization and management (communications technology).

Additional Information TGSA offers two ways to earn a master's degree: 1) via online courses, or 2) via tutorial format. In simplified terms, the tutorial master's program is a self-paced, one-on-one instructional program, whereas the online master's is more like a structured, traditional class. All PhDs are offered in the tutorial format. Online master's courses cost $845 per course; the tutorial format costs $1,995 per quarter. PhD programs cost $2,895 per quarter. Other fees apply.

HARVARD UNIVERSITY

ID	33	**Web Site**	http://icg.harvard.edu/~dep
Type	Private	**E-mail**	dep@fas.harvard.edu
Established		**Toll-Free**	
Regional Accreditation	Yes	**Phone**	617-496-4836
Other Valid Accreditation	Yes	**Fax**	
State Approved	Yes		
Financial Aid	No	**Address**	The Distance Education Program
Total Students			Harvard University
Online/DL Students			Science Center 906
Undergrad Cr. Hr. Cost	See below		1 Oxford Street
Grad Cr. Hr. Cost			Cambridge, MA 02138

☑ **General Courses**	Yes		❏ **Master's**	No
❏ **Certificates**	No		Master's Hours	
❏ **Associate**	No		Master's Cost	
Associate Hours			❏ **PhD**	No
Associate Cost			PhD Hours	
❏ **Bachelor's**	No		PhD Cost	
Bachelor's Hours			❏ **Residency**	None
Bachelor's Cost				

Programs and Courses Harvard offers courses only in the following areas at this time: Approximations, Differential Equations and Integration, the Integral, Integration of Multivariable Functions, Differentiation of Multivariable Functions, and the Derivative. Tuition per two-unit course is $345.

Additional Information Other fees apply. Harvard is one of the most prestigious universities in the United States.

HERIOT-WATT UNIVERSITY

ID	34	**Web Site**	http://www.wcc-eun.com/heriotwatt	
Type	Private	**E-mail**	EUNGrad@aol.com	
Established	1821	**Toll-Free**	800-225-3276	
Regional Accreditation		**Phone**	541-482-5871	
Other Valid Accreditation	Yes	**Fax**	541-482-7544	
State Approved	Yes			
Financial Aid	No	**Address**	Electronic University Network	
Total Students			1977 Colestin Road	
Online/DL Students	15,000		Hombrook, CA 96044	
Undergrad Cr. Hr. Cost				
Grad Cr. Hr. Cost	See below			

❏ **General Courses**	No	☑ **Master's**	Yes
❏ **Certificates**	No	Master's Hours	36
❏ **Associate**	No	Master's Cost	$8,865
Associate Hours		❏ **PhD**	No
Associate Cost		PhD Hours	
❏ **Bachelor's**	No	PhD Cost	
Bachelor's Hours		❏ **Residency**	None
Bachelor's Cost			

Programs and Courses This program is ranked as one of the world's best MBA programs. The program can be done as independent study or with online instructor guidance. The program requires the completion of nine courses. Each course costs $985.

Additional Information Additional costs apply for software and exam fees. For more information, contact Electronic University Network. Heriot-Watt University operates under a Royal Charter from the Queen of England, as do other Accredited British universities. (The Royal Charter is the British equivalent of regional accreditation in the United States.)

THE HOME EDUCATION NETWORK

ID	35	**Web Site**	http://www.then.com
Type	Private	**E-mail**	theninfo@then.com
Established	1993	**Toll-Free**	800-784-8436
Regional Accreditation	Yes	**Phone**	310-825-9971
Other Valid Accreditation	Yes	**Fax**	310-206-3223
State Approved	Yes		
Financial Aid	No	**Address**	The Home Education Network
Total Students			924 Westwood Boulevard,
Online/DL Students	1,100		Suite 650
Undergrad Cr. Hr. Cost	See below		Los Angeles, CA 90024
Grad Cr. Hr. Cost			

☑ **General Courses**	Yes	❏ **Master's**	No
☑ **Certificates**	Yes	Master's Hours	
❏ **Associate**	No	Master's Cost	
Associate Hours		❏ **PhD**	No
Associate Cost		PhD Hours	
❏ **Bachelor's**	No	PhD Cost	
Bachelor's Hours		❏ **Residency**	None
Bachelor's Cost			

Programs and Courses Since 1996, THEN has distributed 135 online courses through UCLA Extension, the nation's largest single-campus continuing higher education program. The following certificate and sequenced programs are now available online: Award in General Business Studies, Cross-Cultural Language and Academic Development Program, Program in Teaching English as a Foreign Language, Program in Online Teaching, and Pre-MBA Skills and Test Preparation Program. Other courses are available in business and management; computers and information systems; education; humanities, sciences, and social sciences; and writing.

Additional Information Courses run approximately $300 to $500 per course, and are priced between $81 and $150 per unit. Duration of courses vary, but most are six weeks.

INTERNATIONAL UNIVERSITY

ID	36	**Web Site**	http://www.international.edu
Type	Private	**E-mail**	info@international.edu
Established		**Toll-Free**	800-777-6463
Regional Accreditation		**Phone**	303-784-8045 ext 8044
Other Valid Accreditation	Yes	**Fax**	
State Approved			
Financial Aid	Yes	**Address**	International University
Total Students			PO Box 6512
Online/DL Students			Englewood, CO 80155-6512
Undergrad Cr. Hr. Cost	See below		
Grad Cr. Hr. Cost	See below		

☑ **General Courses**	Yes	☑ **Master's**	Yes
☑ **Certificates**	Yes	Master's Hours	35
❑ **Associate**	No	Master's Cost	$8,167
Associate Hours		❑ **PhD**	No
Associate Cost		PhD Hours	
☑ **Bachelor's**	Yes	PhD Cost	
Bachelor's Hours	60	❑ **Residency**	None
Bachelor's Cost	$12,000		

Programs and Courses Undergraduate: BA completion degree in which students complete the last 60 credit hours of a 120-credit-hour degree program in business communication. Graduate: MA degree in business communication. Students can also enroll in individual courses or earn one of several certificates of specialization.

Additional Information Three-credit course (bachelor's level) is $600, three-credit course (master's level) is $700, two-credit course (MA capstone course) is $467. Other fees apply. International University is seeking formal accreditation from the United States' regional accreditation agency, North Central Association (NCA) of Colleges and Schools.

ISIM UNIVERSITY

ID	37	Web Site	http://www.isimu.edu
Type	Private	E-mail	admissions@isimu.edu
Established	1953	Toll-Free	800-441-4746
Regional Accreditation		Phone	303-333-4224
Other Valid Accreditation	Yes	Fax	303-336-1144
State Approved	Yes		
Financial Aid	No	Address	ISIM University
Total Students			501 South Cherry Street,
Online/DL Students	350		Room 350
Undergrad Cr. Hr. Cost			Denver, CO 80222
Grad Cr. Hr. Cost	$375		

☑ General Courses	Yes	☑ Master's	Yes
❑ Certificates	No	Master's Hours	36
❑ Associate	No	Master's Cost	$13,500
Associate Hours		❑ PhD	No
Associate Cost		PhD Hours	
❑ Bachelor's	No	PhD Cost	
Bachelor's Hours		❑ Residency	None
Bachelor's Cost			

Programs and Courses ISIM (International School of Information Management) offers an MS in information management and an MBA. Books, software, and other fees add an additional $2,400 to the total cost of the master degrees. In addition to the graduate programs, ISIM offers corporate training programs and classes for continuing education in a number of career-enhancing courses for the professional adult.

Additional Information ISIM was awarded first place in distance learning via the Internet by the U.S. Distance Learning Association (USDLA). Offers some financial aid (not a participant in the Federal Financial Aid Program). For financial aid call 800-477-4977.

KANSAS STATE UNIVERSITY

ID	38	Web Site	http://www.dce.ksu.edu
Type	Public	E-mail	info@dce.ksu.edu
Established	1863	Toll-Free	800-622-2578
Regional Accreditation	Yes	Phone	785-532-5686
Other Valid Accreditation	Yes	Fax	785-532-5637
State Approved	Yes		
Financial Aid	No	Address	Kansas State University
Total Students			Division of Continuing Education
Online/DL Students			13 College Court Building
Undergrad Cr. Hr. Cost	See below		Manhattan, KS 66506-6001
Grad Cr. Hr. Cost	See below		

☑ General Courses	Yes	☑ Master's	Yes
☑ Certificates	Yes	Master's Hours	
❑ Associate	No	Master's Cost	
Associate Hours		❑ PhD	No
Associate Cost		PhD Hours	
☑ Bachelor's	Yes	PhD Cost	
Bachelor's Hours		☑ Residency	Short-term
Bachelor's Cost			

Programs and Courses Students may complete the last two years of a BS in interdisciplinary social science, animal sciences and industry, or dietetics via distance education. Course fees are set by the Kansas Board of Regents and vary from year to year. Nine hours of the 33-hour master's in agribusiness are available through distance education. The master's program costs $10,000 plus additional fees. Elementary and secondary teachers and administrators are able to complete requirements for an English As a Second Language (ESL) certificate via distance learning.

Additional Information The bachelor's program is oriented toward students who have completed at least 60 hours of college credit from KSU or elsewhere and want to get their bachelor's degree off campus. The distance learning department uses videotaped lectures, audio tapes, the World Wide Web, and the Internet as means of program delivery.

KENNEDY-WESTERN UNIVERSITY

ID	39	**Web Site**	http://www.kw.edu	
Type	Private	**E-mail**		
Established	1984	**Toll-Free**	800-969-6906	
Regional Accreditation		**Phone**	307-635-6709	
Other Valid Accreditation		**Fax**	805-379-1092	
State Approved	Yes			
Financial Aid	No	**Address**	Kennedy-Western University	
Total Students	9,000		200 West 17th Street	
Online/DL Students	9,000		Cheyenne, WY 82001-4412	
Undergrad Cr. Hr. Cost	See below			
Grad Cr. Hr. Cost	See below			

❏ **General Courses**	No	☑ **Master's**	Yes
❏ **Certificates**	No	Master's Hours	
❏ **Associate**	No	Master's Cost	
Associate Hours		☑ **PhD**	Yes
Associate Cost		PhD Hours	
☑ **Bachelor's**	Yes	PhD Cost	
Bachelor's Hours		❏ **Residency**	None
Bachelor's Cost			

Programs and Courses The school offers a variety of bachelor's, master's, and doctorate degrees in the following fields: engineering/computer science, business administration, public administration, education and psychology, and health administration. Contact the school for current tuition rates.

Additional Information Credit for prior education and work experience is available. Many students complete their degree requirements in 12 months. Enrollment is not available to California residents.

LANSING COMMUNITY COLLEGE

ID	40	**Web Site**	http://vcollege.lansing.cc.mi.us
Type	Public	**E-mail**	admissions@alpha.lansing.cc.mi.us
Established	1957	**Toll-Free**	800-644-4522
Regional Accreditation	Yes	**Phone**	517-483-1200
Other Valid Accreditation	Yes	**Fax**	517-483-9668
State Approved	Yes		
Financial Aid	No	**Address**	Lansing Community College
Total Students			PO Box 40010
Online/DL Students			Lansing, MI 48901-7210
Undergrad Cr. Hr. Cost	$105		
Grad Cr. Hr. Cost			

☑ **General Courses**	Yes	❑ **Master's**	No
❑ **Certificates**	No	**Master's Hours**	
☑ **Associate**	Yes	**Master's Cost**	
Associate Hours	60	❑ **PhD**	No
Associate Cost	$6,300	**PhD Hours**	
❑ **Bachelor's**	No	**PhD Cost**	
Bachelor's Hours		❑ **Residency**	None
Bachelor's Cost			

Programs and Courses The Virtual College offers an online general associate degree with a concentration in business. It also offers a number of general courses such as World Philosophies I, Writing, American Political Systems, Introduction to Business, Introduction to Computer Information Systems, Introduction to Psychology, Introduction to Sociology, Introduction to the Internet in Business, Multimedia Home Pages for the WWW, and more.

Additional Information Other fees apply. Residents of Michigan pay $76 per credit hour.

MASSACHUSETTS INSTITUTE OF TECHNOLOGY

ID	41	**Web Site**	http://www-caes.mit.edu
Type	Private	**E-mail**	caes-courses@mit.edu
Established	1865	**Toll-Free**	
Regional Accreditation	Yes	**Phone**	617-253-6128
Other Valid Accreditation	Yes	**Fax**	617-258-8831
State Approved	Yes	**Address**	Advanced Study Program
Financial Aid	No		MIT Center for Advanced
Total Students	20,000		Educational Services
Online/DL Students	70		77 Massachusetts Avenue, Room
Undergrad Cr. Hr. Cost	See below		9-335
Grad Cr. Hr. Cost			Cambridge, MA 02139-4307

☑ **General Courses**	Yes	❑ **Master's**	No
☑ **Certificates**	Yes	Master's Hours	
❑ **Associate**	No	Master's Cost	
Associate Hours		❑ **PhD**	No
Associate Cost		PhD Hours	
❑ **Bachelor's**	No	PhD Cost	
Bachelor's Hours		☑ **Residency**	Short-term
Bachelor's Cost			

Programs and Courses The Center for Advanced Educational Services (CAES) offers various credit and non-credit programs through multimodal distance learning methods. Courses usually last one semester (16 weeks), with an average cost of $4600.

Additional Information MIT is one of the world's outstanding universities. It is organized into five schools that contain twenty-one academic departments. Cost varies depending on the distance learning program selected and the type of academic credit provided.

MICHIGAN STATE UNIVERSITY

ID	42	Web Site	http://www.vu.msu.edu
Type	Public	E-mail	mjosephs@msu.edu
Established	1855	Toll-Free	800-496-4678
Regional Accreditation	Yes	Phone	517-355-1855
Other Valid Accreditation	Yes	Fax	517-432-1649
State Approved	Yes		
Financial Aid	Yes	Address	Michigan State University
Total Students	41,545		East Lansing, MI 48824-0590
Online/DL Students			
Undergrad Cr. Hr. Cost	$390		
Grad Cr. Hr. Cost	$437		

☑ General Courses	Yes	☑ Master's	Yes
☐ Certificates	No	Master's Hours	30
☐ Associate	No	Master's Cost	$13,110
Associate Hours		☐ PhD	No
Associate Cost		PhD Hours	
☐ Bachelor's	No	PhD Cost	
Bachelor's Hours		☑ Residency	Short-term
Bachelor's Cost			

Programs and Courses Michigan State's Virtual University offers a variety of courses in a number of academic fields each semester. A MS in criminal justice with a security management specialization is available completely online. A two-day orientation at the beginning of the program is the only on-campus requirement. Call (517) 355-2197 for more information about the master's program.

Additional Information Residents of Michigan pay lower tuition rates.

NEW JERSEY INSTITUTE OF TECHNOLOGY

ID	43	Web Site	http://www.njit.edu/DL
Type	Private	E-mail	dl@njit.edu
Established	1881	Toll-Free	800-624-9850
Regional Accreditation	Yes	Phone	973-642-7015
Other Valid Accreditation	Yes	Fax	973-596-3203
State Approved	Yes	Address	New Jersey Institute of Technology
Financial Aid	Yes		Office of Distance Learning
Total Students	7,700		Guttenberg Information Tech-
Online/DL Students			nologies Center, Suite 5600
Undergrad Cr. Hr. Cost	$381		University Heights
Grad Cr. Hr. Cost	$479		Newark, NJ 07102-1982

☑ General Courses	Yes		☑ Master's	Yes
☑ Certificates	Yes		Master's Hours	36
❑ Associate	No		Master's Cost	$17,244
Associate Hours			❑ PhD	No
Associate Cost			PhD Hours	
☑ Bachelor's	Yes		PhD Cost	
Bachelor's Hours	134		❑ Residency	None
Bachelor's Cost	$51,054			

Programs and Courses Undergraduate: BS computer science (134 credits) or BA information systems (129 credits). Graduate: MS information systems (36 credits) or MS engineering management (30 credits). Graduate certificates: object-oriented design (12 credits), programming environment tools (12 credits), telecommunications networking (12 credits), project management (12 credits), health care information systems (12 credits). NJIT also offers select undergraduate and graduate courses in a variety of fields.

Additional Information Additional fees apply for DL students. In-state residents pay lower fees than those shown above. Video tape leasing is also available to DL students.

NEW SCHOOL FOR SOCIAL RESEARCH

ID	44	**Web Site**	http://www.dialnsa.edu
Type	Private	**E-mail**	dialexec@dialnsa.edu
Established	1919	**Toll-Free**	
Regional Accreditation	Yes	**Phone**	212-229-5880
Other Valid Accreditation	Yes	**Fax**	212-989-2928
State Approved	Yes		
Financial Aid	No	**Address**	The DIAL Office
Total Students	4,000		68 Fifth Avenue, Suite 3
Online/DL Students	1,000		New York, NY 10011
Undergrad Cr. Hr. Cost	See below		
Grad Cr. Hr. Cost	See below		

☑ **General Courses**	Yes	☑ **Master's**	Yes
❑ **Certificates**	No	**Master's Hours**	
❑ **Associate**	No	**Master's Cost**	
Associate Hours		❑ **PhD**	No
Associate Cost		**PhD Hours**	
☑ **Bachelor's**	Yes	**PhD Cost**	
Bachelor's Hours		❑ **Residency**	None
Bachelor's Cost			

Programs and Courses Distance Instruction for Adult Learning (DIAL), the New School's distance learning program, offers a BA in the liberal arts and social sciences (students must have completed 60 semester credits toward a BA degree at an accredited college or university before applying for admission to the DIAL program). Some courses for the MA in media studies can be taken through DIAL. The school also offers more than 100 courses in various areas, including American Immigrant Experience, An Introduction to Astronomy, An Introduction to Culinary History, An Introduction to Jung, Art of Ancient Mexico and Peru, Basic Photography, Beginning AutoCAD, Beginning QuarkXPress, Computer-Based Management Information Systems, and Poetry Workshop.

Additional Information Tuition varies based on the type of program and whether you are registered for non-credit, general credit, or New School credit.

NEW YORK INSTITUTE OF TECHNOLOGY

ID	45	**Web Site**	http://www.nyit.edu/olc	
Type	Private	**E-mail**	olc@acl.nyit.edu	
Established	1955	**Toll-Free**	800-222-6948	
Regional Accreditation	Yes	**Phone**	516-348-3059	
Other Valid Accreditation	Yes	**Fax**	516-348-0299	
State Approved	Yes			
Financial Aid	Yes	**Address**	New York Institute of Technology	
Total Students	10,000		Online Campus, Admission	
Online/DL Students	100		PO Box 9029	
Undergrad Cr. Hr. Cost	$245		Central Islip, NY 11722-9029	
Grad Cr. Hr. Cost	$390			

❑ **General Courses**	No	☑ **Master's**	Yes
❑ **Certificates**	No	**Master's Hours**	Varies
❑ **Associate**	No	**Master's Cost**	
Associate Hours		❑ **PhD**	No
Associate Cost		PhD Hours	
☑ **Bachelor's**	Yes	PhD Cost	
Bachelor's Hours	120	❑ **Residency**	None
Bachelor's Cost	$29,400		

Programs and Courses The Online Campus of NYIT offers a 120-credit bachelor of arts in interdisciplinary studies, a 120-credit bachelor of science in interdisciplinary studies, a 120-credit bachelor of science in business administration (management option), and a 128-credit bachelor of science in behavioral sciences (options: psychology, sociology, community mental health, and criminal justice).

Additional Information NYIT has expanded its online program into the graduate division with the introduction of eight MBA courses as the first step towards a fully integrated Web-based MBA. A master's of professional studies in human relations is also available. Contact the school for more information.

NEW YORK UNIVERSITY

ID	46	Web Site	http://www.sce.nyu.edu/virtual/
Type	Private	E-mail	sce.virtual@nyu.edu
Established	1831	Toll-Free	
Regional Accreditation	Yes	Phone	212-998-7190
Other Valid Accreditation	Yes	Fax	212-995-3656
State Approved	Yes		
Financial Aid	Yes	Address	NYU School of Continuing
Total Students	60,000		Education
Online/DL Students			7 East 12th Street
Undergrad Cr. Hr. Cost			11th Floor
Grad Cr. Hr. Cost	See below		New York, NY 10003-4475

☑ General Courses	Yes		☑ Master's	Yes	
☑ Certificates	Yes		Master's Hours	36	
☐ Associate	No		Master's Cost	$20,817	
Associate Hours			☐ PhD	No	
Associate Cost			PhD Hours		
☐ Bachelor's	No		PhD Cost		
Bachelor's Hours			☐ Residency	None	
Bachelor's Cost					

Programs and Courses NYU's Virtual College offers two online graduate programs—a 36-credit master's of science degree in management control and systems and a 16-credit advanced professional certificate (APC) in information technology. The cost for these programs is $692 for the first credit; each additional credit is $575.

Additional Information The School of Continuing Education also offers several online courses that typically run 10 to 12 sessions and cost $300 to $600. Examples of courses include The Elements of Fiction Writing and Credit Analysis. For a list of current courses, visit http://www.sce.nyu.edu/on-line.

NORTHWESTERN COLLEGE

ID	47	**Web Site**	http://www.nc.edu/virtual
Type	Private	**E-mail**	info@nc.edu
Established	1929	**Toll-Free**	
Regional Accreditation	Yes	**Phone**	419-227-3141
Other Valid Accreditation	Yes	**Fax**	
State Approved	Yes		
Financial Aid	Yes	**Address**	Northwestern's Virtual College
Total Students	2,300		1441 North Cable Road
Online/DL Students	200		Lima, OH 45805
Undergrad Cr. Hr. Cost	$125		
Grad Cr. Hr. Cost			

☑ **General Courses**	Yes	☐ **Master's**	No
☐ **Certificates**	No	Master's Hours	
☑ **Associate**	Yes	Master's Cost	
Associate Hours	108	☐ **PhD**	No
Associate Cost	$13,500	PhD Hours	
☐ **Bachelor's**	No	PhD Cost	
Bachelor's Hours		☐ **Residency**	None
Bachelor's Cost			

Programs and Courses The college offers associate degrees in the following areas: accounting, administrative assistant, agribusiness marketing/management technology, automotive management, business administration, computer technology, legal assisting, legal secretarial, marketing, medical office assistant technology, medical secretarial, travel management, and pharmacy assistant technology.

Additional Information After students complete their associate degree, Virtual College students can go on to receive their bachelor's degree online with Franklin University, Thomas Edison State College, or the University of Phoenix.

NORWICH UNIVERSITY

ID	48	**Web Site**	http://www.norwich.edu/newcollege/
Type	Private	**E-mail**	vcadmis@norwich.edu
Established	1834	**Toll-Free**	800-336-6794
Regional Accreditation	Yes	**Phone**	802-828-8500
Other Valid Accreditation	Yes	**Fax**	
State Approved	Yes		
Financial Aid	Yes	**Address**	Vermont College
Total Students			Norwich University
Online/DL Students			36 College Street
Undergrad Cr. Hr. Cost	See below		Montpelier, VT 05602
Grad Cr. Hr. Cost			

❏ **General Courses**	No	❏ **Master's**		No
❏ **Certificates**	No	Master's Hours		
❏ **Associate**	No	Master's Cost		
Associate Hours		❏ **PhD**		No
Associate Cost		PhD Hours		
☑ **Bachelor's**	Yes	PhD Cost		
Bachelor's Hours	120	☑ **Residency**		Short-term
Bachelor's Cost				

Programs and Courses New College at Norwich University awards the BA degree in liberal studies. Semesters in New College last 18 weeks. Each semester begins with a two-week residency on the Vermont College campus in Montpelier, Vermont. The comprehensive fee for New College is $4,500 per semester for 12 or 15 credits. This fee includes tuition, room and board on the Vermont College campus, and New College Net charges. This price does not include travel costs, books, or the laptop computer.

Additional Information All students must purchase a laptop computer through Norwich University. The laptop computer costs approximately $2,400. With the New College laptop, students can live and work anywhere in the world, attending on-line seminars and learning as they go from their experiences.

NOVA SOUTHEASTERN UNIVERSITY

ID	49	Web Site	http://www.nova.edu
Type	Private	E-mail	amys@sbe.nova.edu
Established	1964	Toll-Free	800-541-6682
Regional Accreditation	Yes	Phone	954-262-7300
Other Valid Accreditation	Yes	Fax	
State Approved	Yes		
Financial Aid	Yes	Address	Nova Southeastern University
Total Students	15,000		3301 College Avenue
Online/DL Students	5,000		Fort Lauderdale, FL 33314
Undergrad Cr. Hr. Cost			
Grad Cr. Hr. Cost	Varies		

❑ General Courses	No	☑ Master's	Yes
❑ Certificates	No	Master's Hours	
❑ Associate	No	Master's Cost	
Associate Hours		☑ PhD	Yes
Associate Cost		PhD Hours	
❑ Bachelor's	No	PhD Cost	
Bachelor's Hours		☑ Residency	Short-term
Bachelor's Cost			

Programs and Courses Awards a number of online degrees, including the MS and EdD programs in Instructional Technology and Distance Education and the EdD program in Child and Youth Studies. The School of Computer and Information Science offers master's degree programs via the Internet, including the MS in computer information systems, computer science, computing technology in education, and management information systems. Certain PhD courses are partially available online. The Virtual MBA program is designed to be completed entirely online with the exception of a one-week class, which is offered at various times throughout the year on campus. Visit the school's Web site or call for more information on courses, degrees, and fees.

Additional Information The largest independent university in Florida, NSU has offices in more than 21 states and in the Bahamas, Jamaica, Panama, Germany, Alberta, and British Columbia.

OHIO UNIVERSITY

ID	50	**Web Site**	http://www.cats.ohiou.edu/
Type	Public		~adullear/esp.htm
Established	1804	**E-mail**	extdegprog@ouvaxa.cats.ohiou.edu
Regional Accreditation	Yes	**Toll-Free**	800-444-2420
Other Valid Accreditation	Yes	**Phone**	614-593-2150
State Approved	Yes	**Fax**	614-593-0452
Financial Aid	No	**Address**	External Student Program
Total Students	19,200		Adult Learning Services
Online/DL Students	5,000		301 Tupper Hall
Undergrad Cr. Hr. Cost	See below		Athens, OH 45701
Grad Cr. Hr. Cost			

☑ **General Courses**	Yes	❏ **Master's**	No
☑ **Certificates**	Yes	Master's Hours	
☑ **Associate**	Yes	Master's Cost	
Associate Hours	Varies	❏ **PhD**	No
Associate Cost		PhD Hours	
☑ **Bachelor's**	Yes	PhD Cost	
Bachelor's Hours	128	❏ **Residency**	None
Bachelor's Cost			

Programs and Courses The External Student Program allows you to complete coursework without coming to campus by using services offered through the office of lifelong learning. AA, AS, associate of applied business (AAB), and associate of individualized studies (AIS). Also bachelor of specialized studies (BSS).

Additional Information The OU College of Business also offers an innovative, project-based MBA degree program for working professionals that combines intensive short residencies with Internet-based learning and collaborative interaction. For information, call: 614-593-2073 or http://oumba.cob.ohiou.edu/~oumba. Courses by correspondence cost $60 per quarter hour. Other fees apply.

OPEN UNIVERSITY

ID	51	**Web Site**	http://www.open.ac.uk
Type	Public	**E-mail**	CREL-GEN@open.ac.uk
Established	1969	**Toll-Free**	
Regional Accreditation		**Phone**	+44 1908 27406
Other Valid Accreditation	Yes	**Fax**	+44 1908 6537
State Approved			
Financial Aid	No	**Address**	Open University
Total Students	218,000		Walton Hall
Online/DL Students	218,000		Milton Keynes
Undergrad Cr. Hr. Cost			MK6AA
Grad Cr. Hr. Cost			United Kingdom

☑ **General Courses**	Yes	☑ **Master's**	Yes
☑ **Certificates**	Yes	Master's Hours	
☑ **Associate**	Yes	Master's Cost	
Associate Hours		☑ **PhD**	Yes
Associate Cost		PhD Hours	
☑ **Bachelor's**	Yes	PhD Cost	
Bachelor's Hours		☑ **Residency**	Short-term
Bachelor's Cost			

Programs and Courses OpenU is Britain's largest educational organization. Teaching materials are delivered to the students in their own homes or places of work by mail, computer, and national BBC broadcasts. Awards BA and BSc degrees, diplomas and certificates, post-graduate certificate in education, MBA, taught higher degrees, and research-based higher degrees. The Open University is accredited in the UK and internationally.

Additional Information You must live in the UK to be able to participate in any of the programs. Recently, Florida State University (see page 129) was offering a master's degree in collaboration with Open University for US residents.

THE PENNSYLVANIA STATE UNIVERSITY

ID	52	**Web Site**	http://www.cde.psu.edu/de
Type	Public	**E-mail**	psude@cde.psu.edu
Established	1855	**Toll-Free**	800-252-3592
Regional Accreditation	Yes	**Phone**	814-865-5403
Other Valid Accreditation	Yes	**Fax**	814-865-3290
State Approved	Yes		
Financial Aid	No	**Address**	The Pennsylvania State University
Total Students	77,318		Department of Distance Education
Online/DL Students	18,000		207 Mitchell Building
Undergrad Cr. Hr. Cost	$115		University Park, PA 16802-3601
Grad Cr. Hr. Cost			

☑ **General Courses**	Yes	❑ **Master's**	No
☑ **Certificates**	Yes	Master's Hours	
☑ **Associate**	Yes	Master's Cost	
Associate Hours	Varies	❑ **PhD**	No
Associate Cost		PhD Hours	
☑ **Bachelor's**	Yes	PhD Cost	
Bachelor's Hours		❑ **Residency**	None
Bachelor's Cost			

Programs and Courses Certificates available in administration of justice; business management; human resources; dietary manager; children, youth, and family services; nurse management; adult development and aging services; paralegal; and business logistics. Associate degrees available in business administration; sociology; letters, arts, and sciences; and dietetic food systems management.

Additional Information A bachelors of liberal studies (BLS) degree is offered as a partnership between Penn State and the University of Iowa.

PURDUE UNIVERSITY

ID	53	**Web Site**	http://www2.mgmt.purdue.edu/
Type	Public		Exceed/EMS/index.html
Established	1869	**E-mail**	custserv@adpc.purdue.edu
Regional Accreditation	Yes	**Toll-Free**	
Other Valid Accreditation	Yes	**Phone**	765-494-7700
State Approved	Yes	**Fax**	765-494-0862
Financial Aid	No		
Total Students	35,156	**Address**	Purdue University
Online/DL Students	100		1310 Krannert Center, Suite 239
Undergrad Cr. Hr. Cost			West Lafayette, IN 47907-1310
Grad Cr. Hr. Cost	See below		

❑ **General Courses**	No	☑ **Master's**	Yes
❑ **Certificates**	No	Master's Hours	48
❑ **Associate**	No	Master's Cost	$33,000
Associate Hours		❑ **PhD**	No
Associate Cost		PhD Hours	
❑ **Bachelor's**	No	PhD Cost	
Bachelor's Hours		☑ **Residency**	Short-term
Bachelor's Cost			

Programs and Courses Offers the Krannert Executive Master of Science in Management (MSE). Residency is six two-week sessions on campus. Duration of the MBA program is two years. The cost of the entire program is $33,000.

Additional Information Purdue's tuition ranks third lowest among Big Ten public schools.

REGIS UNIVERSITY

ID	54	**Web Site**	http://www.MBAREGIS.com
Type		**E-mail**	mba@mbaregis.com
Established	1877	**Toll-Free**	800-622-7344
Regional Accreditation	Yes	**Phone**	
Other Valid Accreditation	Yes	**Fax**	813-628-6124
State Approved	Yes		
Financial Aid	No	**Address**	Regis University
Total Students	8,000		External MBA Program
Online/DL Students			3333 Regis Boulevard
Undergrad Cr. Hr. Cost			Denver, CO 80211-1099
Grad Cr. Hr. Cost	$335		

❑ **General Courses**	No	☑ **Master's**	Yes
❑ **Certificates**	No	Master's Hours	30
❑ **Associate**	No	Master's Cost	$10,050
Associate Hours		❑ **PhD**	No
Associate Cost		PhD Hours	
❑ **Bachelor's**	No	PhD Cost	
Bachelor's Hours		❑ **Residency**	None
Bachelor's Cost			

Programs and Courses You can complete the 10 MBA courses in two years.

Additional Information Books and materials for each course are purchased separately at $195 per course.

ROGERS STATE UNIVERSITY

ID	55	Web Site	http://www.wcc-eun.com/rogers
Type	Public	E-mail	euncouncil@aol.com
Established	1919	Toll-Free	800-225-3276
Regional Accreditation	Yes	Phone	541-482-5871
Other Valid Accreditation	Yes	Fax	541-482-7544
State Approved	Yes		
Financial Aid	Yes	Address	Rogers University
Total Students			Will Rogers & College Hill
Online/DL Students	1,500		Claremore, OK 74017-2099
Undergrad Cr. Hr. Cost	$165		
Grad Cr. Hr. Cost			

☑ General Courses	Yes		❑ Master's	No
❑ Certificates	No		Master's Hours	
☑ Associate	Yes		Master's Cost	
Associate Hours	60–62		❑ PhD	No
Associate Cost	$9,900–$10,230		PhD Hours	
❑ Bachelor's	No		PhD Cost	
Bachelor's Hours			❑ Residency	None
Bachelor's Cost				

Programs and Courses Rogers University is a public, four-year school. It is part of the Oklahoma State System of Higher Education. AA in business administration, humanities, liberal arts; AS in computer science.

Additional Information Rogers State offers courses for credit, taught by regular faculty, through the Electronic University Network. Courses include videotapes produced at KRSC-TV, the university's educational television station, online work with the instructors and other students, as well as productions from other telecourse-producing colleges. Registration is handled through Electronic University Network (see page 126).

SALVE REGINA UNIVERSITY

ID	56	Web Site	http://www.wcc-eun.com/salve
Type	Private	E-mail	eungrad@aol.com
Established	1934	Toll-Free	800-225-3276
Regional Accreditation	Yes	Phone	541-482-5871
Other Valid Accreditation	Yes	Fax	541-482-7544
State Approved	Yes		
Financial Aid	Yes	Address	Electronic University Network
Total Students	2,200		1977 Colestin Road
Online/DL Students	200		Hornbrook, CA 96044
Undergrad Cr. Hr. Cost			
Grad Cr. Hr. Cost	$300		

❏ General Courses	No	☑ Master's	Yes
❏ Certificates	No	Master's Hours	36
❏ Associate	No	Master's Cost	$10,800
Associate Hours		❏ PhD	No
Associate Cost		PhD Hours	
❏ Bachelor's	No	PhD Cost	
Bachelor's Hours		☑ Residency	Short-term
Bachelor's Cost			

Programs and Courses Graduate: MA in international relations, MA in human development.

Additional Information Registration is handled through Electronic University Network (see page 126). Other fees apply.

SOUTHWEST MISSOURI STATE UNIVERSITY

ID	57	**Web Site**	http://www.mscis.smsu.edu
Type	Public	**E-mail**	mscis@mail.smsu.edu
Established	1905	**Toll-Free**	888-879-7678
Regional Accreditation	Yes	**Phone**	417-836-4131
Other Valid Accreditation	Yes	**Fax**	417-836-6907
State Approved	Yes	**Address**	Master of Science in CIS Program
Financial Aid	Yes		CIS Department, 359 Glass Hall
Total Students	17,000		Southwest Missouri State
Online/DL Students			University
Undergrad Cr. Hr. Cost			901 S. National Avenue
Grad Cr. Hr. Cost	$395		Springfield, MO 65804-0089

☑ **General Courses**	Yes		☑ **Master's**	Yes
❏ **Certificates**	No		Master's Hours	36
❏ **Associate**	No		Master's Cost	$14,220
Associate Hours			❏ **PhD**	No
Associate Cost			PhD Hours	
❏ **Bachelor's**	No		PhD Cost	
Bachelor's Hours			☑ **Residency**	Short-term
Bachelor's Cost				

Programs and Courses Graduate: MS in computer information systems (36 credit hours). Residents pay $295 per credit hour. This cost includes tuition, fees, books, and some meals during on-campus sessions.

Additional Information The school is also developing an online MS in administrative studies. SMSU began offering other Internet-based courses in 1998, including organizational communication, religion and human culture, and management of information systems. For information on these courses, visit http://smsuonline.smsu.edu/.

SOUTHWEST UNIVERSITY

ID	58	**Web Site**	http://www.southwest.edu
Type	Private	**E-mail**	southwest@southwest.edu
Established	1984	**Toll-Free**	800-433-5923
Regional Accreditation		**Phone**	504-468-2900
Other Valid Accreditation		**Fax**	504-468-3213
State Approved	Yes		
Financial Aid	No	**Address**	Southwest University
Total Students	500		2200 Veterans Boulevard
Online/DL Students	500		Kenner (New Orleans), LA 70062
Undergrad Cr. Hr. Cost	See below		
Grad Cr. Hr. Cost	See below		

☑ **General Courses**	Yes		☑ **Master's**	Yes
☐ **Certificates**	No		Master's Hours	30–48
☐ **Associate**	No		Master's Cost	
Associate Hours			☑ **PhD**	Yes
Associate Cost			PhD Hours	30
☑ **Bachelor's**	Yes		PhD Cost	
Bachelor's Hours	120		☐ **Residency**	None
Bachelor's Cost				

Programs and Courses BA in psychology; BS, MS, or PhD in criminal justice; BS or PhD in business administration; BA, MA, or PhD in health services administration; master of public administration; master of social work; MS or PhD in education; MBA; MA in counseling/hypnotherapy; MA or PhD in counseling psychology; PhD in administrative studies; PhD in business administration. Additional courses available. Contact the school for tuition information.

Additional Information The school allows students to pay tuition in installments. Currently seeking accreditation from DETC. The term of enrollment for each degree program is 24 consecutive months from the date of enrollment. Credit is granted for work experience and military service. The school has an open enrollment policy. Students may begin studies at any time.

STRAYER COLLEGE

ID	59	Web Site	http://www.strayerdl.edu
Type	Private	E-mail	psb@ns1.strayer.edu
Established	1892	Toll-Free	800-422-8055
Regional Accreditation	Yes	Phone	703-339-1856
Other Valid Accreditation	Yes	Fax	703-339-1852
State Approved	Yes		
Financial Aid	Yes	Address	Strayer Distance Learning Center
Total Students	9,000		8382-F Terminal Road
Online/DL Students			Lorton, VA 22079
Undergrad Cr. Hr. Cost	$180		
Grad Cr. Hr. Cost	$250		

☑ General Courses	Yes		❏ Master's	No
❏ Certificates	No		Master's Hours	
❏ Associate	No		Master's Cost	
Associate Hours			❏ PhD	No
Associate Cost			PhD Hours	
❏ Bachelor's	No		PhD Cost	
Bachelor's Hours			❏ Residency	None
Bachelor's Cost				

Programs and Courses Strayer distance learning courses are designed for those students who desire to integrate academic study with their professional lives in order to enhance their careers or to accomplish personal goals. Selected undergraduate and graduate courses are available online in accounting, business, computer information systems, economics, and general studies.

SUNY EMPIRE STATE COLLEGE

ID	60	**Web Site**	http://www.esc.edu
Type	Public	**E-mail**	cdl@sescva.esc.edu
Established	1991	**Toll-Free**	800-847-3000
Regional Accreditation	Yes	**Phone**	518-587-2100
Other Valid Accreditation	Yes	**Fax**	518-587-2660
State Approved	Yes		
Financial Aid	Yes	**Address**	Center for Distance Learning
Total Students			SUNY Empire State College
Online/DL Students			Two Union Avenue
Undergrad Cr. Hr. Cost	See below		Saratoga Springs, NY 12866-4390
Grad Cr. Hr. Cost			

☑ **General Courses**	Yes	❏ **Master's**	No
☑ **Certificates**	Yes	Master's Hours	
☑ **Associate**	Yes	Master's Cost	
Associate Hours	Varies	❏ **PhD**	No
Associate Cost		PhD Hours	
☑ **Bachelor's**	Yes	PhD Cost	
Bachelor's Hours	Varies	❏ **Residency**	None
Bachelor's Cost			

Programs and Courses The Center for Distance Learning offers a wide range of courses in business, management, arts, sciences, humanities, social sciences, public affairs, technology, communications, and human services. Associate and bachelor's degrees are available in the areas of community and human services, interdisciplinary studies, and business and management. Clusters of courses are available in areas such as fire service administration, health administration, and criminal justice.

Additional Information Cost is $113 per credit for matriculated students and $137 per credit for nonmatriculated students. Course materials average $100 to $125 per course.

TROY STATE UNIVERSITY–FLORIDA REGION

ID	61	**Web Site**	http://www.tsufl.edu
Type	Public	**E-mail**	jkwheeler@tsufl.edu
Established	1887	**Toll-Free**	
Regional Accreditation	Yes	**Phone**	850-301-2151
Other Valid Accreditation	Yes	**Fax**	850-301-2167
State Approved	Yes		
Financial Aid	Yes	**Address**	TSU Distance Education Office
Total Students	3,500		PO Box 2829
Online/DL Students			Fort Walton Beach, FL 32549-2829
Undergrad Cr. Hr. Cost	$113		
Grad Cr. Hr. Cost	$173		

☑ **General Courses**	Yes		☑ **Master's**	Yes
☐ **Certificates**	No		Master's Hours	
☐ **Associate**	No		Master's Cost	
Associate Hours			☐ **PhD**	No
Associate Cost			PhD Hours	
☑ **Bachelor's**	Yes		PhD Cost	
Bachelor's Hours			☐ **Residency**	None
Bachelor's Cost				

Programs and Courses TSU distance learning courses provide students the opportunity to complete a college degree. These asynchronous courses require students to utilize computers, Internet communication, facsimile, or the telephone to interact with faculty and other students. Undergraduate courses are offered in accounting, criminal justice, economics, English, history, math, business, and sociology. Graduate courses are offered in education, history, management, and political science.

Additional Information Troy State uses the quarter-hour system.

UNIVERSITY OF BRIDGEPORT

ID	62	**Web Site**	http://www.bridgeport.edu
Type	Private	**E-mail**	ubonline@cse.bridgeport.edu
Established	1927	**Toll-Free**	800-470-7307
Regional Accreditation	Yes	**Phone**	203-576-4851
Other Valid Accreditation	Yes	**Fax**	203-576-4672
State Approved	Yes		
Financial Aid	Yes	**Address**	Office of Distance Education
Total Students	2,200		University of Bridgeport
Online/DL Students	40		126 Park Avenue
Undergrad Cr. Hr. Cost			Bridgeport, CT 06601-2449
Grad Cr. Hr. Cost	$320		

❑ **General Courses**	No	☑ **Master's**	Yes
❑ **Certificates**	No	Master's Hours	31
❑ **Associate**	No	Master's Cost	$9,920
Associate Hours		❑ **PhD**	No
Associate Cost		PhD Hours	
❑ **Bachelor's**	No	PhD Cost	
Bachelor's Hours		❑ **Residency**	None
Bachelor's Cost			

Programs and Courses Graduate: UB offers an MS in human nutrition. The goal of the Human Nutrition program is to provide a biochemical and physiologically sound understanding of human nutrition and its role in health and disease.

Additional Information Other fees apply. For financial aid information, call (203) 576-4567.

UNIVERSITY OF CALIFORNIA–LOS ANGELES

ID	63	Web Site	http://www.unex.ucla.edu
Type	Public	E-mail	
Established	1917	Toll-Free	
Regional Accreditation	Yes	Phone	310-825-9971
Other Valid Accreditation	Yes	Fax	310-206-3223
State Approved	Yes		
Financial Aid	No	Address	UCLA Extension
Total Students			Westwood/Extension Building
Online/DL Students	300		10995 Le Conte Avenue
Undergrad Cr. Hr. Cost	See below		Los Angeles, CA 90024
Grad Cr. Hr. Cost			

☑ General Courses	Yes	❑ Master's	No
☑ Certificates	Yes	Master's Hours	
❑ Associate	No	Master's Cost	
Associate Hours		❑ PhD	No
Associate Cost		PhD Hours	
❑ Bachelor's	No	PhD Cost	
Bachelor's Hours		❑ Residency	None
Bachelor's Cost			

Programs and Courses UCLA Extension, in association with The Home Education Network (THEN), offers more than 50 courses that you can access online via computer and modem. Courses are offered in the areas of business and management, education, the humanities, entertainment studies and performing arts, and writing. Most courses are three to five units and range from $400 to $500.

Additional Information For a list of certified and sequenced programs offered by UCLA Extension and THEN, see page 133.

UNIVERSITY OF HOUSTON

ID	64	Web Site	http://www.uh.edu/academics/de
Type	Public	E-mail	advisor@uh.edu
Established	1927	Toll-Free	800-687-8488
Regional Accreditation	Yes	Phone	281-395-2800
Other Valid Accreditation	Yes	Fax	281-395-2629
State Approved	Yes		
Financial Aid	Yes	Address	University of Houston
Total Students	31,000		Division of Continuing Education
Online/DL Students	1,000		4242 S. Mason Road
Undergrad Cr. Hr. Cost	$320		Katy, TX 77450
Grad Cr. Hr. Cost	$320		

❑ General Courses	No	☑ Master's	Yes
❑ Certificates	No	Master's Hours	Varies
❑ Associate	No	Master's Cost	
Associate Hours		❑ PhD	No
Associate Cost		PhD Hours	
☑ Bachelor's	Yes	PhD Cost	
Bachelor's Hours	Varies	☑ Residency	Short-term
Bachelor's Cost			

Programs and Courses Undergraduate degrees in computer drafting design, English, Earth science, computer engineering and technology, psychology, hotel and restaurant management, and industrial supervision. Graduate degrees: electrical engineering, hospitality management, computer science, reading specialist certificate, engineering management, training and development, and reading and language arts.

Additional Information University of Houston's award-winning distance education program delivers courses online or via video and television broadcast. Synchronous classes participate in scheduled, real-time sessions with the instructor and/or other class members. Proctored exams are arranged as needed. Texas residents pay $112 per credit hour. Other fees apply.

UNIVERSITY OF MINNESOTA

ID	65	Web Site	http://www.cee.umn.edu/dis
Type	Public	E-mail	instudy@maroon.tc.umn.edu
Established	1909	Toll-Free	800-234-6564
Regional Accreditation	Yes	Phone	612-624-0000
Other Valid Accreditation	Yes	Fax	612-626-7900
State Approved	Yes		
Financial Aid	Yes	Address	Independent and Distance Learning
Total Students			University of Minnesota
Online/DL Students			45 Wesbrook Hall
Undergrad Cr. Hr. Cost	Varies		77 Pleasant Street SE
Grad Cr. Hr. Cost			Minneapolis, MN 55455

☑ General Courses	Yes		☐ Master's	No
☑ Certificates	Yes		Master's Hours	
☐ Associate	No		Master's Cost	
Associate Hours			☐ PhD	No
Associate Cost			PhD Hours	
☑ Bachelor's	Yes		PhD Cost	
Bachelor's Hours			☑ Residency	Short-term
Bachelor's Cost				

Programs and Courses The university offers hundred of college courses with convenient schedules and creative learning resources, including e-mail, videos, World Wide Web technologies, and computer courseware. You may apply IDL courses toward the bachelor of applied business degree or the organizational and professional communication certificate. Courses may apply to other degree and certificate programs, including self-designed degrees in the Inter-College Program or the Program for Individualized Learning, and you may fulfill requirements for degrees at the University and other schools with IDL courses (check first with an adviser). Certificates: liberals arts, science, engineering, accounting, business administration, credit and financial management, and industrial relations. A bachelor of electrical engineering through distance education (BEEDE) is available online.

Additional Information The university uses the quarter hour as the basis of credit evaluation. Limited financial aid is available for distance students.

UNIVERSITY OF NORTH DAKOTA

ID	66	**Web Site**	http://www.space.edu
Type	Public	**E-mail**	borysewi@badlands.nodak.edu
Established		**Toll-Free**	800-828-4274
Regional Accreditation	Yes	**Phone**	701-777-2480
Other Valid Accreditation	Yes	**Fax**	701-777-3711
State Approved	Yes		
Financial Aid	No	**Address**	The Department of Space Studies
Total Students			PO Box 9008, University of North
Online/DL Students			Dakota
Undergrad Cr. Hr. Cost			Grand Forks, ND 58202
Grad Cr. Hr. Cost	$272		

☑ **General Courses**	Yes		☑ **Master's**	Yes
❑ **Certificates**	No		Master's Hours	32
❑ **Associate**	No		Master's Cost	$8,704
Associate Hours			❑ **PhD**	No
Associate Cost			PhD Hours	
❑ **Bachelor's**	No		PhD Cost	
Bachelor's Hours			☑ **Residency**	Short-term
Bachelor's Cost				

Programs and Courses Graduate: MS in space studies. The school offers more than 20 courses in space studies, including Advanced Topics in Space Studies, Earth System Science, and Global Change.

Additional Information Residents of North Dakota pay $102 per credit. Residents of South Dakota, Montana, Saskatchewan, and Manitoba may qualify for reduced tuition.

UNIVERSITY OF PHOENIX

ID	67	**Web Site**	http://www.uophx.edu/online	
Type	Private	**E-mail**		
Established	1976	**Toll-Free**	800-388-5463	
Regional Accreditation	Yes	**Phone**	415-541-0141	
Other Valid Accreditation	Yes	**Fax**		
State Approved	Yes			
Financial Aid	Yes	**Address**	University of Phoenix	
Total Students	42,000		Online Campus	
Online/DL Students	3,000		100 Spear Street, Suite 110	
Undergrad Cr. Hr. Cost	$365		San Francisco, CA 94105	
Grad Cr. Hr. Cost	$460			

☑ **General Courses**	Yes	☑ **Master's**	Yes
☑ **Certificates**	Yes	Master's Hours	51
☑ **Associate**	Yes	Master's Cost	$23,460
Associate Hours	60	❑ **PhD**	No
Associate Cost	$21,900	PhD Hours	
☑ **Bachelor's**	Yes	PhD Cost	
Bachelor's Hours	120–126	❑ **Residency**	None
Bachelor's Cost	$43,800–$45,900		

Programs and Courses AA in general studies; BS in business with majors in management, administration, project management, marketing, or information systems. Graduate: MBA; MBA in global management; MBA in technology management; MS in computer information systems; MA in organizational management. (The MA requires only 41 hours.)

Additional Information The University of Phoenix has an excellent reputation for delivering online graduate programs to students anywhere in the world. It is one of the first universities to start online higher education. Most courses are 3 credit hours and last six weeks. The university is ranked second largest among the top 10 private schools, based on total enrollment. The university gives credit for some work experience.

UNIVERSITY OF WASHINGTON EXTENSION

ID	68	**Web Site**	http://www.edoutreach.
Type	Public		washington.edu/DL
Established	1890	**E-mail**	
Regional Accreditation	Yes	**Toll-Free**	800-543-2320
Other Valid Accreditation	Yes	**Phone**	206-543-2320
State Approved	Yes	**Fax**	206-685-0887
Financial Aid	No	**Address**	University of Washington Extension
Total Students	30,000		Distance Learning
Online/DL Students	12,000		Box 354223
Undergrad Cr. Hr. Cost	Varies		5001 25th Avenue NE
Grad Cr. Hr. Cost			Seattle, WA 98105-4190

☑ **General Courses**	Yes		❑ **Master's**	No
☑ **Certificates**	Yes		Master's Hours	
❑ **Associate**	No		Master's Cost	
Associate Hours			❑ **PhD**	No
Associate Cost			PhD Hours	
❑ **Bachelor's**	No		PhD Cost	
Bachelor's Hours			☑ **Residency**	Short-term
Bachelor's Cost				

Programs and Courses UW Distance Learning offers more than 120 credit and noncredit courses. Credit courses can be applied toward a degree or to prepare for UW admission. Students are mailed study guides and textbooks. Students can communicate with their instructors by mail, e-mail, and voicemail. General courses typically cost $385 each, consist of five quarter credit hours, and cover areas such as English, anthropology, marketing, statistics, and more. The university offers certificates in C programming; C++ programming; writer's program; project management; school library media specialist; public health; and teaching, learning, and technology.

Additional Information Prices vary for the certificate programs. Some certificate programs require short-term residency. Other fees apply.

UNIVERSITY OF WISCONSIN–STOUT

ID	69	**Web Site**	http://major.uwstout.edu
Type	Public	**E-mail**	conted@uwstout.edu
Established	1891	**Toll-Free**	
Regional Accreditation	Yes	**Phone**	715-232-2693
Other Valid Accreditation	Yes	**Fax**	
State Approved	Yes		
Financial Aid	No	**Address**	Office of Continuing Education
Total Students	7,200		University of Wisconsin-Stout
Online/DL Students			140 Vocational Rehabilitation Bldg
Undergrad Cr. Hr. Cost			PO Box 790
Grad Cr. Hr. Cost			Menomonie, WI 54751-0790

☑ **General Courses**	Yes	❑ **Master's**	No
☑ **Certificates**	Yes	Master's Hours	
❑ **Associate**	No	Master's Cost	
Associate Hours		❑ **PhD**	No
Associate Cost		PhD Hours	
❑ **Bachelor's**	No	PhD Cost	
Bachelor's Hours		❑ **Residency**	None
Bachelor's Cost			

Programs and Courses   The Office of Continuing Education offers a certificate program for members of the Association of Online Professionals using Web-based instructional units. Participants in the AOP Certificate Program use a Web browser to access all instructional content. AOP Certificate Program provides options for "professional" tracks in three content areas: ISP Management Professional, Internet Services Professional, and Web Deployment Professional.

Additional Information   Many UW-Stout credit outreach courses are offered using distance learning technologies, including the World Wide Web, broadcast television and videotapes, and full-motion video. Contact the Office of Continuing Education for a current credit outreach catalog.

VATTEROTT GLOBAL ONLINE

ID	70	**Web Site**	http://www.VatterottGlobal.com
Type	Private	**E-mail**	VattInfo@ponyexpress.net
Established	1969		VattInfo@ccp.com
Regional Accreditation		**Toll-Free**	888-766-3601
Other Valid Accreditation	Yes	**Phone**	816-364-3601
State Approved	Yes	**Fax**	888-546-3616
Financial Aid	No		
Total Students	2500	**Address**	Vatterott Global Online
Online/DL Students			3131 Frederick Avenue
Undergrad Cr. Hr. Cost	See below		St. Joseph, MO 64506
Grad Cr. Hr. Cost			

☑ **General Courses**	Yes		❑ **Master's**	No
☑ **Certificates**	Yes		Master's Hours	
❑ **Associate**	No		Master's Cost	
Associate Hours			❑ **PhD**	No
Associate Cost			PhD Hours	
❑ **Bachelor's**	No		PhD Cost	
Bachelor's Hours			❑ **Residency**	None
Bachelor's Cost				

Programs and Courses A diploma in computer programming and systems analysis is offered online; the program is 60 weeks long and costs $7,200. A variety of computer programming courses are available, including Introduction to Programming, Integrated Software Applications, Visual Basic, Structured Cobol, C Programming, and Management Information Systems. Each course costs $1,200 and lasts 10 weeks. Plans are underway to offer an associate degree in computer programming and network management.

Additional Information The college has 12 physical campuses across the nation. Fees include all additional costs: textbooks, software, compilers, and shipping costs. The college offers one week trial computer and Internet training for newly enrolled students. No financial aid is available for online students at this time, but the college offers a flexible installment payment plan and meets eligibility criteria for Hope and Lifetime tax credit.

VIRTUAL ONLINE UNIVERSITY/
ATHENA UNIVERSITY

ID	71	**Web Site**	http://www.athena.edu
Type	Private	**E-mail**	cipher@vousi.com
Established	1995	**Toll-Free**	
Regional Accreditation		**Phone**	573-874-4107
Other Valid Accreditation		**Fax**	573-442-0699
State Approved	Yes		
Financial Aid	No	**Address**	VOU Services International, Inc.
Total Students			dba Athena University
Online/DL Students			601 W. Nifong Boulevard,
Undergrad Cr. Hr. Cost			Suite 5A
Grad Cr. Hr. Cost	$700		Columbia, MO 65203

❏ **General Courses**	No		☑ **Master's**	Yes	
❏ **Certificates**	No		Master's Hours	30	
❏ **Associate**	No		Master's Cost	$21,000	
Associate Hours			❏ **PhD**	No	
Associate Cost			PhD Hours		
❏ **Bachelor's**	No		PhD Cost		
Bachelor's Hours			❏ **Residency**	None	
Bachelor's Cost					

Programs and Courses Athena University is totally online. Graduate: MBA, with the emphasis of the integration of technology and management strategies. The program can be completed in 12 to 18 months.

Additional Information The degree will be issued by Ecole Superieure de Commerce-Pau (ESCP). ESCP is ranked this year in the top five schools in France in international programs. ESCP is accredited by the Conference de Grandes Ecoles, an elite association of business and engineering schools in France. Cost of the program is $21,000; cost per semester credit hour and number of master's hours are based on the total cost of the program and its duration.

WALDEN UNIVERSITY

ID	72	**Web Site**	http://www.waldenu.edu
Type	Private	**E-mail**	info@waldenu.edu
Established	1970	**Toll-Free**	800-925-3368
Regional Accreditation	Yes	**Phone**	612-338-7224
Other Valid Accreditation	Yes	**Fax**	612-338-5092
State Approved	Yes		
Financial Aid	Yes	**Address**	Walden University
Total Students			155 Fifth Avenue South
Online/DL Students			Minneapolis, MN 55401
Undergrad Cr. Hr. Cost			
Grad Cr. Hr. Cost	See below		

❑ **General Courses**	No	☑ **Master's**	Yes
❑ **Certificates**	No	Master's Hours	30
❑ **Associate**	No	Master's Cost	$9,900
Associate Hours		☑ **PhD**	Yes
Associate Cost		PhD Hours	Varies
❑ **Bachelor's**	No	PhD Cost	See below
Bachelor's Hours		☑ **Residency**	Short-term
Bachelor's Cost			

Programs and Courses MS in educational change and technology innovation ($330 per credit hour); PhD in applied management and decision sciences, education, health services, human services, and psychology. All PhDs but psychology cost $3,040 per quarter. PhD in psychology costs $285 per quarter credit hour (most psychology courses are 5 credits each).

Additional Information Doctoral students are required to fulfill an academic residency requirement. Residency periods are dispersed throughout the calendar year and throughout the United States to accommodate the students.

Appendix:
Nationally Recognized
Accrediting Agencies and Associations

The following regional and national accrediting agencies and associations are recognized by the US Secretary of Education as reliable authorities concerning the quality of education or training offered by the institutions of higher education or higher education programs they accredit. The dates specified for each entry are the date of initial listing as a nationally recognized agency or association, the date of the most recent grant of renewed recognition based on the Advisory Committee's last full review of the agency, and the date of the agency's next scheduled review for renewal of recognition.

The Accrediting Agency Evaluation Branch does not maintain a list of accredited institutions. For current accreditation information regarding individual institutions or their programs, please contact the appropriate accrediting agency from the list below.

Regional Institutional Accrediting Association

Connecticut, Maine, Massachusetts, New Hampshire, Rhode Island, Vermont

New England Association of Schools and Colleges
(1952/1992/1997)

> Vincent Ferrandino, Executive Director
> 209 Burlington Road
> Bedford, MA 01730-1433
> **Phone:** (617) 271-0022
> **Fax:** (617) 271-0950

Commission on Institutions of Higher Education
New England Association of Schools and Colleges
Charles Cook, Director
209 Burlington Road
Bedford, MA 01730-1433

Commission on Vocational, Technical, Career Institutions
New England Association of Schools and Colleges
Richard Mandeville, Director
209 Burlington Road
Bedford, MA 01730-1433

Regional Institutional Accrediting Commissions

Delaware, District of Columbia, Maryland, New Jersey, New York, Pennsylvania, Puerto Rico, Virgin Islands

Commission on Higher Education
Middle States Association of Colleges and Schools
(1952/1996/2001)

Jean Avent Morse, Executive Director
3624 Market Street
Philadelphia, PA 19104
Phone: (215) 662-5606
Fax: (215) 662-5950

Commission on Secondary Schools
Middle States Association of Colleges and Schools
(1988/1996/1998)

Joseph J. DeLucia, Executive Director
3624 Market Street
Philadelphia, PA 19104
Phone: (215) 662-5606
Fax: (215) 662-5905

Arizona, Arkansas, Colorado, Illinois, Indiana, Iowa, Kansas, Michigan, Minnesota, Missouri, Nebraska, New Mexico, North Dakota, Ohio, Oklahoma, South Dakota, West Virginia, Wisconsin, Wyoming

Commission on Institutions of Higher Education
North Central Association of Colleges and Schools
(1952/1992/1997)

Patricia A.Thrash, Executive Director
30 North LaSalle Street, Suite 2400
Chicago, IL 60602
Phone: (312) 263-0456 or (800) 621-7440
Fax: (312) 263-7462

Commission on Schools
North Central Association of Colleges and Schools
(1974/1992/1997)

Kenneth F. Gose, Executive Director
Arizona State University
Tempe, Arizona 85287-3011
Phone: (800) 525-9517
Fax: (602) 965-9423

Alaska, Idaho, Montana, Nevada, Oregon, Utah, Washington

Commission on Colleges
Northwest Association of Schools and Colleges
(1952/1992/1997)

Sandra E. Elman, Executive Director
11130 NE 33rd Place, Suite 120
Seattle, Washington 98004
Phone: (206) 827-2005
Fax: (206) 827-3395

Alabama, Florida, Georgia, Kentucky, Louisiana, Mississippi, North Carolina, South Carolina, Tennessee, Texas, Virginia

Commission on Colleges
Southern Association of Colleges and Schools
(1952/1995/1999)

James T. Rogers, Executive Director
1866 Southern Lane
Decatur, GA 30033-4097
Phone: (404) 679-4501 ext. 512 or (800) 248-7701
Fax: (404) 679-4558

California, Hawaii, American Samoa, Guam, and the Commonwealth of the Northern Mariana Islands

Accrediting Commission for Community and Junior Colleges
Western Association of Schools and Colleges
(1952/1992/1997)

David B. Wolf, Executive Director
3402 Mendocino Avenue
Santa Rosa, CA 95403
Phone: (707) 569-9177
Fax: (707) 569-9179

Accrediting Commission for Schools
Western Association of Schools and Colleges
(1974/1995/1999)

Donald G. Haught, Executive Director
533 Airport Boulevard, Suite 200
Burlingame, CA 94010
Phone: (415) 696-1060
Fax: (415) 375-7790

Accrediting Commission for Senior Colleges and Universities
Western Association of Schools and Colleges
(1952/1995/1998)

Ralph Wolff, Executive Director
c/o Mills College, Box 9990
Oakland, CA 94613-0990
Phone: (510) 632-5000
Fax: (510) 632-8361

National Institutional and Specialized Accrediting Bodies

ACUPUNCTURE

First professional master's degree and professional master's level certificate and diploma programs in acupuncture and Oriental medicine:

National Accreditation Commission for Schools and Colleges of
Acupuncture and Oriental Medicine
(1988/1995/1999)

Dort S. Bigg, Executive Director
1010 Wayne Avenue, Suite 1270
Silver Spring, MD 20910
Phone: (301) 608-9680
Fax: (301) 608-9576

ALLIED HEALTH, GENERAL

Private, postsecondary institutions offering allied health education:

Accrediting Bureau of Health Education Schools
(1982/1995/1998)

> Carol Moneymaker, Administrator
> 2700 South Quincy Street, Suite 210
> Arlington, VA 22206
> **Phone:** (703) 998-1200
> **Fax:** (703) 998-2550

ALLIED HEALTH, OTHER

Health education programs for the following:

> Cytotechnologist
> Diagnostic Medical Sonographer
> Electroneurodiagnostic Technologist
> Emergency Medical Technician-Paramedic
> Perfusionist
> Physician Assistant
> Respiratory Therapist and Respiratory Therapy Technician
> Surgical Technologist

Commission on Accreditation of Allied Health Education Programs
(1952/1996/1998)

> L. M. Detmer, Secretary
> 35 East Wacker Drive, Suite 1970
> Chicago, IL 60601-2208
> **Phone:** (312) 553-9355
> **Fax:** (312) 553-9616

The Commission on Accreditation of Allied Health Education Programs (CAAHEP) is recognized as a coordinating agency for accreditation of education for the allied health occupations listed above. In carrying out its accreditation activities, CAAHEP cooperates with the Committees on Accreditation sponsored by various allied health and medical specialty organizations. For information concerning the cooperating review committee, refer to the disciplines as listed separately. Other allied health disciplines accredited by agencies recognized by the department outside the aegis of CAAHEP are listed elsewhere in this appendix.

Cytotechnology (CAAHEP)

Programs for the cytotechnologist:

Cytotechnology Programs Review Committee
American Society of Cytopathology
(1974/1996/1998)

> Shirley Indictor, Secretary
> 400 West 9th Street, Suite 201
> Wilmington, DE 19801
> **Phone:** (302) 429-8802
> **Fax:** (302) 429-8807

Diagnostic Medical Sonography (CAAHEP)

Programs for the diagnostic medical sonographer:

Joint Review Committee on Education in Diagnostic Medical Sonography *(sponsored by the American College of Cardiology, the American College of Radiology, the American Institute of Ultrasound in Medicine, the American Society of Echocardiography, the American Society of Radiologic Technologists, the Society of Diagnostic Medical Sonographers, and the Society of Vascular Technology)*
(1983/1996/1998)

> Annamarie Dubies-Appel, Executive Director
> 7108-C South Alton Way
> Englewood, CO 80112-2901
> **Phone:** (303) 694-6191
> **Fax:** (303) 741-3655

Electroneurodiagnostic Technology (CAAHEP)

Programs for the electroneurodiagnostic technologist:

Joint Review Committee on Education in Electroneurodiagnostic Technology *(sponsored by the American Electroencephalographic Society and the American Society of Electroneurodiagnostic Technologists)*
(1983/1996/1998)

> Becky Appenzeller, Executive Secretary
> Route 1, Box 62 A
> Genoa, WI 54632
> **Phone:** (608) 689-2058
> **Fax:** None

Emergency Medical Services (CAAHEP)

Programs for the emergency medical technician-paramedic:

Joint Review Committee on Educational Programs for the EMT-Para-medic *(sponsored by the American College of Emergency Physicians, the American College of Surgeons, the American Society of Anesthesiologists, the National Association of Emergency Medical Technicians, the National Registry of Emergency Medical Technicians, the American College of Cardiology, the American Academy of Pediatrics, and the National Council of State EMS Coordinators)* *(1983/1996/1998)*

> Annamarie Dubies-Appel, Executive Secretary
> 7108-C South Alton Way, Suite 150
> Englewood, CO 80112-2106
> **Phone:** (303) 694-6191
> **Fax:** (303) 741-3655

Perfusion (CAAHEP)

Programs for the perfusionist:

Accreditation Committee for Perfusion Education *(sponsored by the American Association for Thoracic Surgery, the American Board of Cardiovascular Perfusion, the American Society of Extracorporeal Technology, and the Society of Thoracic Surgeons, Society of Cardiovascular Anesthesiologists, the Perfusion Program Directors Council)* *(1983/1996/1998)*

> Annamarie Dubies-Appel, Executive Director
> 7108-C South Alton Way
> Englewood, CO 80112-2106
> **Phone:** (303) 694-6191
> **Fax:** (303) 741-3655

Physician Assistant Education (CAAHEP)

Programs for the physician assistant:

Accreditation Review Committee on Education for Physician Assistant *(sponsored by the American Academy of Family Physicians, the American Academy of Pediatrics, the American Academy of Physician Assistants, the American College of Physicians, the American College of Surgeons, and the Association for Physician Assistant Programs, the American Medical Association)* *(1974/1996/1998)*

John E. McCarty, Executive Director
1000 North Oak Avenue
Marshfield, WI 54449-5788
Phone: (715) 389-3785
Fax: (715) 389-3131

Respiratory Therapy (CAAHEP)

Programs for the respiratory therapist and respirator therapy technician:

Joint Review Committee for Respiratory Therapy Education *(sponsored by the American College of Chest Physicians, the American Society of Anesthesiologists and the American Thoracic Society) (1974/1996/1998)*

Richard T. Walker, Executive Director
1701 West Euless Boulevard, Suite 300
Euless, TX 76040
Phone: (817) 283-2835 or (800) 874-5615
Fax: (817) 354-8519

Surgical Technology (CAAHEP)

Programs for the surgical technologist:

Accreditation Review Committee for the Surgical Technologist *(sponsored by the American College of Surgeons, the American Hospital Association, and the Association of Surgical Technologists) (1978/1996/1998)*

Annamarie Dubies-Appel, Accreditation Manager
7108 C South Alton Way
Englewood, CO 80112-2106
Phone: (303) 694-6191
Fax: (303) 741-3655

ART AND DESIGN

Degree-granting schools and departments and non-degree granting schools that are predominantly organized to offer education in art, design, or art/design-related disciplines:

Commission on Accreditation
National Association of Schools of Art and Design
(1966/1992/1997)

Samuel Hope, Executive Director
11250 Roger Bacon Drive, Suite 21
Reston, VA 22090
Phone: (703) 437-0700
Fax: (703) 437-6312

BIBLE COLLEGE EDUCATION

Bible colleges and institutes offering undergraduate programs:

Commission on Accrediting
Accrediting Association of Bible Colleges
(1952/1996/2000)

Randall E. Bell, Executive Director
Box 1523
Fayetteville, Arkansas 72702
Phone: (501) 521-8164
Fax: (501) 521-9202

BUSINESS

Private postsecondary schools, junior colleges, and senior colleges that are predominantly organized to educate students for business careers, including master's degree programs in senior colleges of business as well as independent, freestanding institutions offering only graduate business and business-related programs at the master's degree level:

Accrediting Council for Independent Colleges and Schools
(1956/1995/1999)

Stephen D. Parker, Executive Director
750 First Street, NE, Suite 980
Washington, DC 20002-4242
Phone: (202) 336-6780
Fax: (202) 842-2593

CHIROPRACTIC EDUCATION

Programs leading to the DC degree:

Commission on Accreditation
The Council on Chiropractic Education
(1974/1992/1997)

Paul D. Walker, Executive Vice President
7975 North Hayden Road, Suite A-210
Scottsdale, Arizona 85258
Phone: (602) 443-8877
Fax: (602) 483-7333

CHRISTIAN EDUCATION

Christian postsecondary institutions that offer certificates, diplomas, and associate, baccalaureate, and graduate degrees:

Accrediting Commission
Transnational Association of Christian Colleges and Schools
(1991/1996/1999)

Earl A. Mills, Executive Director
PO Box 328
Forest, VA 24551
Phone: (804) 525-9539
Fax: (804) 525-9538

CONTINUING EDUCATION

Non-collegiate continuing education institutions and programs:

Accrediting Commission
Accrediting Council for Continuing Education and Training
(1978/1994/1997)

Roger Williams, Executive Director
1200 Nineteenth Street, NW, Suite 200
Washington, DC 20036
Phone: (202) 955-1113
Fax: (202) 955-1118

COSMETOLOGY

Postsecondary schools and departments of cosmetology arts and sciences:

National Accrediting Commission of Cosmetology Arts and Sciences
(1970/1996/1999)

Mark Gross, Chief Executive Officer
901 North Stuart Street, Suite 900
Arlington, VA 22203
Phone: (703) 527-7600
Fax: (703) 527-8811

CYTOTECHNOLOGY

Commission on Accreditation of Allied Health Education Programs
(See listing under Allied Health, Other.)

DANCE

Institutions and units within institutions offering degree-granting and non-degree-granting programs in dance and dance-related disciplines:

Commission on Accreditation
National Association of Schools of Dance
(1983/1991/1997)

> Samuel Hope, Executive Director
> 11250 Roger Bacon Drive, Suite 21
> Reston, VA 22090
> **Phone:** (703) 437-0700
> **Fax:** (703) 437-6312

DENTAL AND DENTAL AUXILIARY PROGRAMS

Programs leading to the DDS or DMD degree, advanced general dentistry and specialty programs, general practice residency programs and programs in dental hygiene, dental assisting, and dental technology:

Commission on Dental Accreditation
American Dental Association
(1952/1995/2000)

> James J. Koelbl
> Associate Executive Director, Education
> Commission on Dental Accreditation
> American Dental Association
> 211 East Chicago Avenue, 18th Floor
> Chicago, IL 60611
> **Phone:** (312) 440-2500 or (800) 621-8099
> **Fax:** (312) 440-2915

DIAGNOSTIC MEDICAL SONOGRAPHY

Commission on Accreditation of Allied Health Education Programs
(See listing under Allied Health, Other.)

DIETETICS

Coordinated undergraduate programs in dietetics and postbaccalaureate dietetic internships:

Division of Education Accreditation/Approval
The American Dietetic Association
(1974/1996/2000)

> Beverly E. Mitchell, Administrator
> Department of Education, ADA
> 216 West Jackson Blvd., Suite 800
> Chicago, IL 60606-6995
> **Phone:** (312) 899-4872
> **Fax:** (312) 899-1758

DISTANCE EDUCATION AND TRAINING

Home study schools (including associate, baccalaureate, or master's degree-granting home study schools):

Accrediting Commission
Distance Education and Training Council (DETC; formerly the National Home Study Council)
(1959/1996/2000)

> Michael P. Lambert, Executive Secretary
> 1601 18th Street, NW
> Washington, DC 20009
> **Phone:** (202) 234-5100
> **Fax:** (202) 332-1386
> **Web site:** http://www.detc.org
> **E-mail:** detc@detc.org

ELECTRONEURODIAGNOSTIC TECHNOLOGY

Joint Review Committee on Education in Electroneurodiagnostic Technology
(See listing under Allied Health, Other.)

EMERGENCY MEDICAL SERVICES

Joint Review Committee on Educational Programs for the EMT-Paramedic
(See listing under Allied Health, Other.)

ENGINEERING

Basic (baccalaureate) and advanced (master's) level programs in engineering; associate and baccalaureate degree programs in engineering technology; and engineering-related programs at the baccalaureate and advanced degree level:

Accreditation Board for Engineering and Technology, Inc.
(1952/1992/1997)

> George D. Peterson, Executive Director
> 111 Market Place, Suite 1050
> Baltimore, MD 21202
> **Phone:** (410) 347-7700
> **Fax:** (410) 625-2238

ENVIRONMENT

Baccalaureate programs in environmental health science and protection:

National Environmental Health Science and Protection Accreditation Council
(1995/1996/1998)

> Patricia Cancellier, Executive Director
> 6307 Huntover Lane
> Rockville, MD 20852
> **Phone:** (301) 231-5205
> **Fax:** None

FUNERAL SERVICE EDUCATION

Institutions and programs awarding diplomas, associate degrees and bachelor's degrees:

Committee on Accreditation
American Board of Funeral Service Education
(1972/1992/1997)

> Gordon S. Bigelow, Executive Director
> 13 Gurnet Road, #316
> PO Box 1305
> Brunswick, ME 04011
> **Phone:** (207) 798-5801
> **Fax:** (207) 798-5988

HEALTH SERVICES ADMINISTRATION

Graduate programs in health services administration:

Accrediting Commission on Education for Health Services Administration
(1970/1995/2000)

> Patrick M. Sobczak, President
> 1911 North Fort Myer Drive, Suite 503
> Arlington, VA 22209
> **Phone:** (703) 524-0511
> **Fax:** (703) 525-4791

HISTOLOGIC TECHNOLOGY

Programs for the histologic technician/technologist:

National Accrediting Agency for Clinical Laboratory Sciences *(sponsored by the American Society for Medical Technology and the American Society of Clinical Pathologists)*
(1974/1996/1999)

> Cynthia Wells, Chairman
> 8410 West Bryn Mawr Avenue, Suite 670
> Chicago, IL 60631
> **Phone:** (312) 714-8880
> **Fax:** (312) 714-8886

INTERIOR DESIGN

Two-year preprofessional assistant level programs (certificate and associate degree), first professional degree level programs (master's and baccalaureate degree and three-year certificate) and post-professional master's degree programs:

Committee on Accreditation
Foundation for Interior Design Education Research
(1976/1992/1997)

> Kayem Dunn, Executive Director
> 60 Monroe Center, NW, Suite 300
> Grand Rapids, MI 49503-2920
> **Phone:** (616) 458-0400
> **Fax:** (616) 458-0460

JOURNALISM AND MASS COMMUNICATIONS

Units within institutions offering professional undergraduate and graduate (master's) degree programs:

Accrediting Committee
Accrediting Council on Education in Journalism and Mass Communications
(1952/1996/2001)

> Susanne Shaw, Executive Director
> University of Kansas School of Journalism
> Stauffer-Flint Hall
> Lawrence, KS 66045
> **Phone:** (913) 864-3986
> **Fax:** (913) 864-5225

LAW

Professional schools of law:

Council of the Section of Legal Education and Admissions to the Bar
American Bar Association
(1952/1992/1997)

> James P. White
> Consultant on Legal Education, ABA
> Indiana University
> 550 West North Street
> Indianapolis, IN 46202
> **Phone:** (317) 264-8340
> **Fax:** (317) 264-8355

LIBERAL EDUCATION

Institutions of higher education and programs within institutions of higher education that offer liberal arts degree(s) at the baccalaureate level or a documented equivalency:

American Academy for Liberal Education
(1995/1997)

> Jeffrey D. Wallin, President
> 1015 18th Street, NW, Suite 204
> Washington, DC 20036
> **Phone:** (202) 452-8611
> **Fax:** (202) 452-8620

MARRIAGE AND FAMILY THERAPY

Graduate degree programs and clinical training programs:

Commission on Accreditation for Marriage and Family Therapy Education
American Association for Marriage and Family Therapy
(1978/1995/2000)

> Colleen Peterson, Executive Director
> Commission on Accreditation
> 1133 15th Street, NW, Suite 300
> Washington, DC 20005-2710
> **Phone:** (202) 452-0109
> **Fax:** (202) 232-2329

MEDICAL LABORATORY TECHNICIAN EDUCATION

Schools and programs for the medical laboratory technician:

Accrediting Bureau of Health Education Schools
(See listing under Allied Health, General.)

Associate degree and certificate programs for the medical laboratory technician:

National Accrediting Agency for Clinical Laboratory Sciences
(See listing under Histologic Technology.)

MEDICAL TECHNOLOGY

Professional programs:

National Accrediting Agency for Clinical Laboratory Sciences
(See listing under Histologic Technology.)

MEDICINE

Programs leading to the MD degree:

Liaison Committee on Medical Education of the Council on Medical Education of the American Medical Association and the American Medical Colleges
(1952/1991/1997)

The LCME is administered in odd-numbered years, beginning each July 1, by:

Harry S. Jonas, Secretary, LCME
American Medical Association
515 North State Street
Chicago, IL 60610
Phone: (312) 464-4657
Fax: (312) 464-5830

The LCME is administered in even-numbered years, beginning each July 1, by:

Donald G. Kassebaum, Secretary, LCME
Association of American Medical Colleges
2450 N Street, NW
Washington, DC 20037
Phone: (202) 828-0596
Fax: (202) 828-1125

MONTESSORI EDUCATION

Montessori teacher education programs and institutions:

Montessori Accreditation Council for Teacher Education
(1995/1997)

Sandi McDonald-West, Acting Executive Director
Montessori Accreditation Council for Teacher Education
225 South Lake Avenue
Pasadena, CA 91101
Phone: (817) 488-2138
Fax: (817) 566-1640

MUSIC

Institutions and units within institutions (including community/junior colleges and independent degree-granting institutions) offering degree-granting and non-degree-granting programs in music and music-related disciplines:

Commission on Accreditation
Commission on Non-Degree-Granting Accreditation
Commission on Community/Junior College Accreditation
National Association of Schools of Music
(1952/1992/1997)

Samuel Hope, Executive Director
11250 Roger Bacon Drive, Suite 21
Reston, VA 22090
Phone: (703) 437-0700
Fax: (703) 437-6312

NATUROPATHY

Programs leading to the ND or NMD degree:

Council on Naturopathic Medical Education
(1987/1995/1999)

Robert Lofft, Executive Director
PO Box 11426
Eugene, OR 97440-3626
Phone: (541) 484-6028
Fax: None

NUCLEAR MEDICINE TECHNOLOGY

Programs for the nuclear medicine technologist:

Joint Review Committee on Educational Programs in Nuclear Medicine Technology
(1974/1995/1999)

Elaine Cuklanz, Executive Director
1144 West 3300 South
Salt Lake City, UT 84119-3330
Phone: (801) 975-1144
Fax: (801) 975-7872

NURSE ANESTHETISTS

Generic nurse anesthesia educational programs/schools:

Council on Accreditation of Nurse Anesthesia Educational Programs
American Association of Nurse Anesthetists
(1955/1996/2001)

Betty J. Horton, Director of Accreditation
222 South Prospect, Suite 304
Park Ridge, IL 60068-4010
Phone: (847) 692-7050
Fax: (847) 693-7137

NURSE-MIDWIVES

Basic certificate and graduate nurse-midwifery education programs for registered nurses, as well as the accreditation and preaccreditation of pre-certification nurse-midwifery education programs:

Division of Accreditation
American College of Nurse-Midwives
(1982/1995/2000)

> Helen Varney Burst, Chair
> Division of Accreditation
> Nurse-Midwifery Program
> 818 Connecticut Avenue, NW, Suite 900
> Washington, DC 20006
> **Phone:** (202) 728-9877
> **Fax:** (202) 728-9897

NURSE PRACTITIONERS

Women's health nurse practitioners' programs located within the United States and US territories:

Council on Accreditation
National Association of Nurse Practitioners in Reproductive Health
(1996/1998)

> Susan Wysocki, Executive Director
> 2401 Pennsylvania Avenue, NW, Suite 350
> Washington, DC 20027-1718
> **Phone:** (202) 466-4825
> **Fax:** (202) 466-3826

NURSING

Programs in practical nursing, and diploma, associate, baccalaureate, and higher degree nurse education programs:

Board of Review for Baccalaureate and Higher Degree Programs
Board of Review for Diploma Programs
Board of Review for Practical Nursing Programs
Board of Review for Associate Degree Programs
National League for Nursing, Inc.
(1952/1995/1997)

Patricia Moccia, Chief Executive Officer
350 Hudson Street
New York, NY 10014
Phone: (800) 669-1656
Fax: (212) 989-3710

OCCUPATIONAL EDUCATION

Private, postsecondary degree and non-degree-granting institutions that are predominantly organized to educate students for trade, occupational, or technical careers:

Accrediting Commission of Career Schools and Colleges of Technology
(1967/1995/1999)

Thomas A. Kube, Executive Director
2101 Wilson Boulevard, Suite 302
Arlington, VA 22201
Phone: (703) 247-4212
Fax: (202) 842-2585

Non-degree-granting postsecondary occupational/vocational institutions and those postsecondary occupational/vocational education institutions currently accredited by the following agency that either have state authorization to grant the applied associate degree in specific vocational/occupational fields at the present time or that receive such authorization during the current two-year recognition period:

Council on Occupational Education (formerly the Commission on Occupational Education Institutions of the Southern Association of Colleges and Schools)
(1969/1995/1997)

Harry L. Bowman, Executive Director
41 Perimeter Center East, NE, Suite 640
Atlanta, GA 30346
Phone: (770) 396-3898 or (800) 917-2081
Fax: (770) 396-3790

OCCUPATIONAL THERAPY

Professional Programs:

Accreditation Committee
American Occupational Therapy Association
(1952/1995/2000)

Brena Manoly, Acting Director
Accreditation Department
4720 Montgomery Lane
PO Box 31220
Bethesda, MD 20824-1220
Phone: (301) 652-2682
Fax: (301) 652-7711

OPTICIANRY

Two-year programs for the ophthalmic dispenser and one-year programs for the ophthalmic laboratory technician:

Commission on Opticianry Accreditation
(1985/1992/1997)

Floyd H. Holmgrain, Jr., Executive Director
10111 Martin Luther King, Jr. Highway, Suite 100
Bowie, MD 20720-4299
Phone: (301) 459-8075
Fax: (301)577-3880

OPTOMETRY

Professional optometric degree programs, optometric residency programs, and optometric technician programs:

Council on Optometric Education
American Optometric Association
(1952/1992/1997)

Joyce Urbeck, Manager
243 North Lindbergh Boulevard
St. Louis, MO 63141
Phone: (314) 991-4100
Fax: (314) 991-4101

OSTEOPATHIC MEDICINE

Programs leading to the DO degree:

Bureau of Professional Education
American Osteopathic Association
(1952/1995/2000)

Conrad Retz, Interim Secretary
Department of Education
142 East Ontario Street
Chicago, IL 60611
Phone: (312) 280-5800
Fax: (312) 280-3860

PASTORAL EDUCATION

Basic, advanced, and supervisory clinical pastoral education programs:

Accreditation Commission
Association for Clinical Pastoral Education, Inc.
(1969/1991/1997)

Russell H. Davis, Executive Director
1549 Claremont Road, Suite 103
Decatur, GA 30033
Phone: (404) 320-1472
Fax: None

PERFUSION

Accreditation Committee for Perfusion Education
(See listing under Allied Health, Other.)

PHARMACY

Professional degree programs:

American Council on Pharmaceutical Education
(1952/1995/2000)

Daniel A. Nona, Executive Director
311 West Superior
Chicago, IL 60610
Phone: (312) 664-3575
Fax: (312) 664-4652

PHYSICAL THERAPY

Professional programs for the physical therapist and programs for the physical therapist assistant:

Commission on Accreditation in Education
American Physical Therapy Association
(1977/1996/2001)

Virginia Nieland, Director
Department of Accreditation
Trans Potomac Plaza
1111 North Fairfax Street
Alexandria, VA 22314
Phone: (703) 684-3245
Fax: (703) 684-7344

PHYSICIAN ASSISTANT EDUCATION

Accreditation Review Committee on Education for Physician Assistant
(See listing under Allied Health, Other.)

PODIATRY

Colleges of podiatric medicine, including first professional and graduate degree programs:

Council on Podiatric Medical Education
American Podiatric Medical Association
(1952/1995/2000)

Jay Levrio, Director
9312 Old Georgetown Road
Bethesda, MD 20814-2752
Phone: (301) 571-9200
Fax: (301) 530-2752

PSYCHOLOGY

Doctoral programs in clinical, counseling, school and combined pro-
fessional-scientific psychology, and predoctoral internship programs
in professional psychology:

Committee on Accreditation
American Psychological Association
(1970/1992/1997)

Paul Nelson, Administrative Officer of Accreditation
750 First Street, NE
Washington, DC 20002-4242
Phone: (202) 336-5979
Fax: (202) 336-5978

PUBLIC HEALTH

Graduate schools of public health and graduate programs offered outside schools of public health in community health education and in community health/preventive medicine:

Council on Education for Public Health
(1974/1992/1997)

>   Patricia Evans, Executive Director
>   1015 15th Street, NW, Suite 403
>   Washington, DC 20005
>   **Phone:** (202) 789-1050
>   **Fax:** (202) 289-8274

RABBINICAL AND TALMUDIC EDUCATION

Advanced rabbinical and Talmudic schools:

Accreditation Commission
Association of Advanced Rabbinical and Talmudic Schools
(1974/1992/1997)

>   Bernard Fryshman, Executive Vice-President
>   175 Fifth Avenue, Room 711
>   New York, NY 10010
>   **Phone:** (212) 477-0950
>   **Fax:** (212) 533-5335

RADIOLOGIC TECHNOLOGY

Educational programs for radiographer and radiation therapists:

Joint Review Committee on Education in Radiologic Technology
(1957/1995/1999)

>   Marilyn Fay, Executive Director
>   20 North Wacker Drive, Suite 900
>   Chicago, IL 60606-2901
>   **Phone:** (312) 704-5300
>   **Fax:** (312) 704-5304

RESPIRATORY THERAPY

Joint Review Committee for Respiratory Therapy Education
(See listing under Allied Health, Other.)

SPEECH-LANGUAGE PATHOLOGY AND AUDIOLOGY

Master's degree programs:

American Speech-Language Hearing Association
(1967/1991/1997)

> Sharon Goldsmith, Director
> Academic Affairs and Credentialing Division
> 10801 Rockville Pike
> Rockville, MD 20852
> **Phone:** (301) 897-5700
> **Fax:** (301) 571-0457

SURGICAL TECHNOLOGY

Accreditation Review Committee for the Surgical Technologist

(See listing under Allied Health, Other.)

TEACHER EDUCATION

Baccalaureate and graduate programs for the preparation of teachers and other professional personnel for elementary and secondary schools:

National Council for Accreditation of Teacher Education
(1952/1995/1999)

> Arthur Wise, President
> 2010 Massachusetts Avenue, NW
> Washington, DC 20036-1023
> **Phone:** (202) 466-7496
> **Fax:** (202) 296-6620

THEATER

Institutions and units within institutions offering degree-granting and/or non-degree-granting programs in theater and theater-related disciplines:

Commission on Accreditation
National Association of Schools of Theater
(1982/1991/1997)

> Samuel Hope, Executive Director
> 11250 Roger Bacon Drive, Suite 21
> Reston, VA 22090
> **Phone:** (703) 437-0700
> **Fax:** (703) 437-6312

THEOLOGY

Freestanding schools, as well as schools affiliated with larger institutions offering graduate professional education for ministry and graduate study of theology:

Commission on Accrediting
Association of Theological Schools in the United States and Canada
(1952/1995/1998)

> James L. Waits, Executive Director
> 10 Summit Park Drive
> Pittsburgh, PA 15275-1103
> **Phone:** (412) 788-6505
> **Fax:** (412) 788-6510

VETERINARY MEDICINE

Colleges of veterinary medicine offering programs leading to a professional degree:

Council on Education
American Veterinary Medical Association
(1952/1992/1997)

> Donald G. Simmons, Director
> Education and Research Division
> 1931 North Meacham Road, Suite 100
> Schaumburg, IL 60173
> **Phone:** (708) 925-8070 or (800) 248-2862
> **Fax:** (708) 925-1329

OTHER

Registration [accreditation] of collegiate degree-granting programs or curriculums offered by institutions of higher education and of credit-bearing certificate and diploma programs offered by degree-granting institutions of higher education:

New York State Board of Regents
(1952/1995/1999)

> Richard Mills, Commissioner of Education
> State Education Department
> Albany, NY 12224
> **Phone:** (518) 474-2593
> **Fax:** (518) 486-2779

Glossary

asynchronous communication: One-way communciation, as when one computer sends information and another computer receives it; digital communication in which there is no timing requirement for transmitting material.

browser: A program that allows you to read hypertext and navigate the World Wide Web. Two well-known browsers are Netscape Navigator and Microsoft Explorer.

e-mail: Electronic mail; messages automatically passed from one computer user to another, often through computer networks and/or via modems over telephone lines.

GB: Gigabyte; one gigabyte can store one billion characters of information.

HTML: Hypertext markup language; the formatting language used on the Web.

hypertext: a collection of documents containing cross-references or "links" which, with the aid of an interactive browser program, allow the reader to move easily from one document to another.

Internet: A network of networks; computers linked together via phone lines, fiber optics, satellites, etc. Also called the Net.

ISP: Internet service provider; an entity that provides Internet access to the public for a fee.

KB: Kilobyte; one kilobyte can store one thousand characters of information.

MB: Megabyte; one megabyte can store one million characters of information.

millisecond: 1/1000 of a second.

modem: A device that enables computers to communicate by converting data over phone lines; may be internal or external. The faster the modem, the more quickly you will send and receive information over the Internet.

quarter credit hour: A quarter credit hour is equal to two-thirds of a semester credit hour.

RAM: Random access memory; the amount of data the computer can hold while in use (the data is usually lost when the machine is turned off). RAM is measured in megabytes (MB): 16 MB of RAM is 16,000,000 characters of information.

search engine: A program that allows you to search for a specific term or subject on the Internet.

semester credit hour: Most colleges and universities rate a semester credit hour equal to one hour of lectures per week for sixteen weeks.

snail mail: Paper mail sent via the postal service as opposed to electronic mail.

synchronous communication: Two-way communication, usually interactive and live (real-time); digital communication in which a common timing signal is established that dictates when individual bits of information can be transmitted.

URL: Uniform resource locator; the address for a page on the Web, such as www.anyuniversity.edu.

voice mail: Programs that allow you to record a voice message and transmit it over the Internet.

Web site: Any computer on the Internet running a World-Wide Web server process. A particular web site is identified by the hostname part of a URL.

World Wide Web: An Internet client-server hypertext distributed information retrieval system. On the World Wide Web everything (documents, menus, indices) is represented to the user as a hypertext object in HTML format. Hypertext links refer to other documents by their URLs. The browser runs on the user's computer and provides two basic navigation operations: to follow a link or to send a query to a server. Also called WWW or the Web.

References

Cady, Glee H. and Pat McGregor. *Mastering the Internet.* San Francisco: Sybex, 1995.

"Council on Competitiveness, May 1993." http://www.si.umich.edu/hp/who (December 5, 1996.)

Ellsworth, Jill H. *Education on the Internet.* Indianapolis: Sam's Publishing, 1994.

Gates, Bill, Nathan Myhrvold, and Peter Rinearson. *The Road Ahead.* Allentown, PA: Viking Penguin, 1995.

Harawitz, Howard. *Web Page Construction Kit.* Bedford, Nova Scotia, Canada: Brooklyn North Software Works, 1995.

Internet Basics: Video Projects. Videocassette. Video Projects, Inc., 1995.

The Internet Show. John Levine and Gina Smith, narrators. Videocassette. Brandenburg Productions, Inc. and The Production Companies, Inc., 1994.

Index

About the Author

SALEH (SAM) ATIEH is a computer and information consultant with eighteen years of international experience. He has designed, programmed, and implemented software applications in various industries. He has worked in Kuwait, India, Egypt, and the United States and served as a computer consultant for the US military. He has taught in his specialty, system design and programming, at a number of US colleges and institutions. He holds a bachelor's degree in computer science from East Texas State University and is completing his master of business administration degree from Northwest Missouri State University in Maryville, Missouri. Currently, he is the Director of Online Education at Vatterott College in St. Joseph, Missouri. He is an active member of the United States Distance Learning Association and International Who's Who of Professionals. Mr. Atieh appreciates any comments or suggestions you might have. Send him e-mail at saleh@ccp.com, visit his Web Site (http://www.SamTech.net), or write him at PO Box 8614, St. Joseph, MO 64508-8614.